MUSICA DISCIPLINA

A YEARBOOK OF THE HISTORY OF MUSIC

Edited by
STANLEY BOORMAN

VOLUME LIX, 2014

American Institute of Musicology

MUSICA DISCIPLINA

A YEARBOOK OF THE HISTORY OF MUSIC

VOLUME LIX, 2014

Edited by

STANLEY BOORMAN

Editorial Board

Tim Carter	University of North Carolina at Chapel Hill, USA
Anthony Cummings	Lafayette College, USA
Mark Everist	University of Southampton, GB
Dinko Fabris	Conservatorio di Bari, Italy
Barbara Haggh-Huglo	University of Maryland, USA
David Hiley	Universität Regensburg, Germany
Karl Kuegle	Universiteit Utrecht, Netherlands
Birgit Lodes	Universität Wien, Austria
Laurenz Luetteken	Universität Zurich, Switzerland
Anne MacNeil	University of North Carolina at Chapel Hill, USA
Anne Smith	Schola Cantorum Basiliensis, Switzerland
Anne Stone	CUNY, USA

AMERICAN INSTITUTE OF MUSICOLOGY

The American Institute of Musicology publishes seven series of critical editions, scholarly studies, reference works, and this journal, all dedicated to the study of the music and culture of the Medieval, Renaissance, and early Baroque eras. The publications of the Institute are used by scholars and performers alike and constitute a major core collection of early music, theoretical writings on music, and the scholarly analysis of that music and its sources.

For information on establishing a standing order or subscription to this journal or any of our series, or for editorial guidelines on submitting proposals, please contact:

American Institute of Musicology
800 736-0070 (U.S. book orders) / 608 836-9000 (phone) / 608 831-8200 (fax)
http://www.corpusmusicae.com
orders@corpusmusicae.com / info@corpusmusicae.com

© 2016 by the American Institute of Musicology, Verlag Corpusmusicae, GmbH. All rights reserved. No part of this journal may be reproduced or transmitted in any form by any electronic or mechanical means (including photocopying, recording, or information storage and retrieval) without permission in writing from the publisher. Offprints of individual articles are available upon request.

ISSN 0077–2461 v. 59

Printed in the United States of America. ♾The paper used in this publication meets the minimum requirements of the American National Standard for Information Sciences Permanence of Paper for Printed Library Materials, ANSI Z39.48-1992.

TABLE OF CONTENTS

Carlo Bosi, Gentils Gallans de France: *The Vicissitudes of a French War Song between Brittany and Rome* 7

Joseph Arthur Mann, "Both Schollers and Practicioners": *The Pedagogy of Ethical Scholarship and Music in Thomas Morley's* Plaine and Easie Introduction to Practicall Musicke 53

Daniele Sabaino and Marco Mangani, *Tonal Space Organization in Josquin's Late Motets* 93

Anne Smith, *Jesuit Imagery, Rhetoric, and Victoria's* Senex Puerum Portabat 127

* * *

Directions to Contributors 159

CONTRIBUTORS

CARLO BOSI is director of the federally-funded project at the Universität Salzburg, "Anleihe und Zitat monophoner Melodien im Lied um 1500." He has published on early Venetian opera and its connections to other arts and to philosophy of the time, and on 15th-century music and theory. He has recently published *Emergence of Modality in Late Medieval Song: The Cases of Du Fay and Binchois*.

JOSEPH ARTHUR MANN is a doctoral candidate and Teaching Fellow at the Catholic University of America. His research focuses on morality, reform, and politics in the music and musical writings of early modern England, in particular on the use of music and the idea of music as propaganda in seventeenth-century England. His secondary research interests include the historiography of music criticism in the nineteenth century.

MARCO MANGANI, formerly a researcher at the Faculty of Musicology of the University of Pavia/Cremonia, is now professor at the Department for Humanities of the University of Ferrara. He has written essays on Renaissance polyphony and on Italian instrumental music of the 18th and 19th centuries, as well as a book on Boccherini.

DANIELE SABAINO is professor of Modality and Medieval Notation at the Department of Musicology and Cultural Heritage of the University of Pavia/Cremona. He has published historical, philological, and analytical essays on music from the Middle Ages to the 17th century, on Juan Caramuel Lobkowitz and on past and present relationships between music and liturgy. He is the editor of Marcantonio Ingegneri's motets in the composer's Collected Works.

ANNE SMITH teaches recorder and transverse flute at the Schola Cantorum Basiliensis. A primary concern involves bridging the gap between knowledge of the writings of 16th-century musical theorists and their application in performance, as reflected in her recent book *The Performance of 16th-Century Music: Learning from the Theorists*. As a logical consequence of this work, she is also investigating the historical sources of 20th-century performance of early music, working on a study to be entitled *Ina Lohr (1903–1983): Transcending the Boundaries of Early Music*.

GENTILZ GALLANS DE FRANCE: THE VICISSITUDES OF A FRENCH WAR SONG BETWEEN BRITTANY AND ROME*

CARLO BOSI

Many years ago, Howard M. Brown demonstrated how late 15th-/early 16th-century French song underwent a profound transformation, largely freeing itself from the strictly formal requirements of the formes fixes of courtly tradition.[1] Not only did the literary topics change (from traditionally 'courtly' to more or less 'popularizing'), but also musical diction mutated from highly melismatic to prevailingly syllabic, with clear-cut, squared melodic phrases. This radical stylistic change is borne out by a growing usage of and interest in thematic and literary materials belonging to a completely different, 'lower' register, which slowly but inexorably dissolves from within the high-brow posture and mood of what has often been termed Franco-Burgundian court song. At first wittily contrasted and stacked up against traditional court forms, such as the combinative chanson[2]—which in its polytextuality and polysemy somehow reveals compositional strategies in common with the late medieval motet—, these melodies and texts ever more frequently receive autonomous arrangements, bringing to life completely new and fresh song styles and forms, and progressively transforming the sophisticated melodic language of late 15th-century song.[3]

---

* This work was supported by the Austrian Science Fund (FWF), within the Research Project P 27257–G18. I would also here like to take the opportunity to thank Bonnie Blackburn, whose insightful and, as always, illuminating comments have nurtured this essay at a time when it was still 'in progress.'

1. Cf., in particular, Brown, "The *Chanson rustique*," and "The Transformation of the Chanson."

2. For the combinative chanson, see in particular the following studies by Maniates: "Combinative Chansons in the Dijon Chansonnier"; "Combinative Chansons in the Escorial Chansonnier"; and *The Combinative Chanson: An Anthology*. For a fresh, intertextual view of combinative song by way of a specific example, see Zazulia, "'Corps contre corps.'"

3. This is not to say, of course, that the old *formes fixes* died out altogether. On the contrary, as has already been shown in several studies, they lived on for some time in the works of composers such as Agricola, la Rue, Prioris, etc., though certainly not much beyond the first few years of the 16th century.

Many of the melodies forming the basis of polyphonic songs (and also masses) in this period have been transmitted in two important monophonic song collections compiled around the turn of the century—F-Pn, f. fr. 9346 (*Bayeux*) and F-Pn, f. fr. 12744 (*Paris 12744*)[4],—indirectly demonstrating that they often 'lead' an existence of their own, independent of their employment within polyphonic textures. This is also revealed by the dissemination of these melodies within different, independent polyphonic arrangements, indirectly witnessing to their diffusion and circulation (at least in part) beyond the generally accepted model of manuscript transmission, and probably relying to a large extent on an oral-memorial pattern. In order to illustrate this, I would like to discuss a specific case of a song based on the combination of two completely different melodies, both found in *Paris 12744*. This song even succeeds in becoming the model of a partly 'imitation,' partly *cantus firmus* mass, while the mass is additionally built on a further pre-existing tune, unrelated to the first one. Additionally I will show how the Italian transmission of the song might be linked to the campaigns of Charles VIII in the peninsula between 1494 and 1495.

Noble Gallants

Songs with the incipit *Gentilz gallans de France*, *Gentilz gallans adventureux*, *Gentilz gallans compaignons* or just *Gentil galans* are transmitted in several Italian and (mostly) French sources. (See Table 1.) Nearly all the Italian sources have, as usual, no more text than the corrupted incipit *Gentil galans* or—in the case of one of the two arrangements in *Canti C numero cento cinquanta* (*Canti C*)—*Gentil galans de gerra*. Only the subsequent transmissions in the Florentine part-books I-CTb MSS 95–6/F-Pn, nouv. acq. fr. 1817 (*Cortona/Paris*), no. 10, with its concordances in the later I-Fn, MSS Magl. XIX, 164–7 (*Florence 164–7*) and I-Fc, MS Basevi 2442 (*Strozzi Chansonnier*), no. 12, carry complete texts in all parts: the former displays a corrupted and, as we shall see, significantly altered version of *Gentilz gallans de France*, with the latter being a very close variant of *Gentilz gallans adventureux*. On the other hand, both text and music of *Gentilz gallans compaignons*, only handed down in *Bayeux*, fols. 46v–47r, seem to be unrelated to the other *Gentil(z)*

---

4. For *Bayeux*, see Gérold, *Le Manuscrit de Bayeux*; and Rahn, "Melodic and Textual Types." For *Paris 12744* see, most recently, Kraft, *Einstimmigkeit um 1500*, which takes issue with many assumptions contained in Rahn's dissertation. From here, sources will be referred to with the abbreviated designations given (in parentheses) at their first citation.

ga(l)lans chansons, although the 'merry-drinking-and-cavorting' song topic somehow connects it with *Gentilz gallans adventureux*. Lastly, a three- and a four-voice composition, each with the incipit *Gentil galans*, and also seemingly independent of the aforementioned songs, are transmitted by I-Fn, MS Banco Rari 229 (*Florence 229*) at, respectively, fols. 132v–133r and 186v–187r, the former with a concordance in I-Fn, MS Magl. XIX, 178 (*Florence 178*)—in both sources attributed to Agricola—the latter being, on the other hand, an anonymous *unicum*. Material from these two compositions, but particularly from the four-voice song, informs Sanctus and Benedictus of the opening mass of V-CVbav, MS Capp. Sist. 41 (*Capp. Sist. 41*), which, however, is based, in all other movements, on the *Gentil(z) ga(l)lans de France/de gerra* setting, as we shall see later.[5] Table 1 charts and numbers the different *Gentil(z) ga(l)lans* songs, with their concordances (sharing a column) and variants (placed horizontally).

Songs **1a** and **2a**[6] appear side by side on a single opening of *Paris 12744*. Apart from the shared modality (authentic D-protus) and the two initial intervals (an ascending minor third followed by a descending minor second), the music of the two pieces does not seem to be closely related, although the descending fifth a'-d' does seem to form the thematic core of the second section of both compositions. The texts of the two monophonic songs, on the other hand, could not show greater contrast, apart from the allusive common incipit. Indeed whereas **2a**, a ballade with the refrain "*Autant en emporte le vent*,"[7] deals with the tricks to be employed (including lying and deceit) for

---

5. The song *Gentil gallans*, attributed to Hayne van Ghizeghem in V-CVbav, MS Capp. Giulia XIII, 27 (*Capp. Giulia*), fols. 74v–75r (81v–82r) with an anonymous concordance in I-Bc Q.17, fols. 17v–18r, has no relationship whatsoever with any of the songs discussed here. This is also remarked by Fallows, in *A Catalogue of Polyphonic Songs*, p. 171, who also provides a short and useful description of the two monophonic chansonniers on pp. 34–35. This specific *Gentil gallans* setting, moreover, though textless beyond the incipit, has a corona at the midpoint, revealing that it must have been a *rondeau*, a *forme fixe*, placing it at a further remove from the 'popularizing' tradition represented by the pieces dealt with in this essay. For a brief discussion of this song, see also Atlas, *The Cappella Giulia Chansonnier*, part 1, 171.

6. From now on we shall refer to the different songs and their arrangements following the numbering in Table 1.

7. Though the refrain text is identical to the first line of a noted chanson by la Rue, the music has only the vaguest resemblance to it, mainly due to the *parlando* rhythm on the words "*Autant en emporte*" (in both cases centred on a') and the rapid descent (a fifth in the monophonic song, a fourth in la Rue's setting, culminating into a cadence, on the words "*le vent*"). La Rue's song is transmitted in B-Br MS 228, fols. 9v–10r, with a concordance in the later I-Fc, MS Basevi 2439, fols. 12v–13r; for a modern edition, see Picker, *The Chanson Albums of Marguerite of Austria*, 204–6, with commentary on 118–19.

Table 1. Gentil(z) ga(l)lans songs with concordances and variants.

1. Gentilz gallans de France				2. Gentilz gallans adventureux		3. Gentilz gallans compaignons	4. Gentil galans	
a. *Paris 12744*, fol. 87, 1v. (D-protus): full text	b. *Canti C*, fols. 14v–15r, Gentil galans de gerra I, 4vv. (G-protus): incipit	c. *Canti C*, Gentil galans de gerra II, fols. 74v–75r, 4vv. (G-protus). Stappen: incipit	d. *Capp. Sist. 41*, fols. 2r–14v, 4vv. (G-protus), Pintelli (in the table of contents): Kyrie–Credo & Osanna–Agnus dei from Missa Gentilz gallans de France: full text and incipit Gentiz gallans de France in Agnus Dei I, bassus	a. *Paris 12744*, fol. 88r, 1v. (D-protus): full text	b. *Canti C*, fols. 43v–44r, 4vv. (G-protus): incipit	*Bayeux*, fols. 46v–47r, 1v. (F-tritus): full text	a. *Florence 229*, fols. 186v–187r, 4vv. (G-protus): incipit	b. *Florence 229*, fols. 132v–133r, 3vv. (G-tetrardus), Alexander Agricola: incipit
Cortona 95–6/Paris 1817, no. 10: corrupted and augmented text		Pernner, pp. 318–19, Prioris: incipit		*Strozzi Chansonnier*, no. 12 [4vv.]: full text			*Florence 178*, fols. 47v–48r, Alexander: incipit	
Florence 164–7, no. 63, 4vv.: corrupted and augmented text								c. *Capp. Sist. 41*, fols. 2v–14r, 4vv. (G-protus), Pintelli (in the table of contents); Sanctus & Benedictus from Missa Gentilz gallans de France: full ordinarium text

the seduction and the erotic fulfilment of young ladies, and for living a carefree, ribald life, **1a** is an anti-Breton war song likely relating to the conflict raging between the Kingdom of France and the Dukedom of Brittany between 1486 and 1488.[8] After the final defeat of the Breton army in 1488, the formal betrothal of Maximilian of Austria with the thirteen-year-old Anne (the eldest daughter and heir presumptive to the late Breton Duke Francis II) in Rennes (1490), and its subsequent rejection, forced in the following year by the French King and his allies, the young Duchess saw no other choice but to acquiesce and, in the end, give her hand in marriage to Charles VIII of France,[9] thus basically sealing the end of the Dukedom's independence (Treaty of Rennes, 1491).[10] In the poem a lady begs some soldiers (indeed, the "*gentilz gallans de France*") to send her greetings to her lover, presently at war; as identifying features she mentions "*la croix blanche, les esperons dorez,*" which were at this time distinguishing marks of the French King's army. At her plea the soldiers reply that she should stop mourning since "*ils est trespassé; Il est mort en Bretaigne, Les Bretons l'ont tué*": these lines further underline that the song represents the French side of the events. As a result, the *gallans* of the two contiguous songs are indeed of two completely different sorts: on the one hand soldiers in service, on the other lusty revellers, as the following texts show:

Paris 12744, fol. 87v: Song 1a
"Gentilz gallans de France,
Qui en la guerre allez,
Je vous prie qu'il vous plaise
Mon amy saluer."
"Comment le saluroye,
Quant point ne le congnois?"
"Il est bon à congnoistre:
Il est de blanc armé.
Il porte la croix blanche,
Les esperons dorez
Et au bout de la lance
Ung fer d'argent doré."

---

8. See Kraft, *Einstimmigkeit um 1500*, included CD.

9. Charles had, in his turn, to send his *fiancée* Margaret of Austria (who, soon after their engagement in 1483, had been living at the French Court) back to her father Maximilian, something which he, apparently, did only half-heartedly and after concerted efforts on the part of his counsellors. See Bulst, "Karl VIII.," 338.

10. Ibid., 336–38.

> "Ne plorés plus la belle,
> Car il est trespassé.
> Il est mort en Bretaigne,
> Les Bretons l'ont tué."
> "Je veü faire sa fouce,
> L'orée d'ung vert pré
> Et veü chanter sa messe
> À quatre cordelliers."

***Paris 12744,* fol. 88r: Song 2a**
Gentilz gallans adventureux,
Qui en amours plaisir prenez,
Monstrés-vous tousjours gracieux
Et saigement vous gouvernez.
S'aucune dame rencontrez,
Pour voz plaisirs, joyeusement,
Donnez dedans, ne vous feignez:
Autant en emporte le vent.
Sy le jeu luy est amoureulx
Tantoust d'elle bien aymé serez,
Tant que vous serez vigoreux
Et que fournir au jeu pourrez.
Vostre jeunesse passerés
À voz plaisirs joyeusement,
De surplus ne vous souciez:
Autant en emporte le vent.
Sy elle est fine, soyez songneux
Que de ses fins tours vous gardez,
Car souvent les plus rouges gueux
Y sont surprins, bien l'entendez.
Sy elle demande, promectez
Et vous ventés fort hardiment:
Que vous est-il se vous mentez?
Autant en emporte le vent.

This ambiguity of connotation is inherent in the French medieval meaning of *gal(l)an*, since the noun/adjective designates both a valiant, intrepid man, maybe an officer of some rank—in this case relevant for fighting soldiers—as well as someone bent on debauchery and sexual and drinking indulgence, the *double entendre* being enhanced by the fact that stationed soldiers were often inclined to all sorts of excesses, including physical violence. The fact that the two songs appear side by side on the same opening seems to be an allusion to this polysemy, thus also indirectly pointing to the scribe's ordering of the manuscript's contents according to some mental and verbal associations. Such a hypothesis is confirmed by other comparable occurrences in the source: see, for example, nos. 107 *Hellas, j'ay perdu la personne* (fol. 72r) and 108 *Hélas, je l'ay perdue* (fols. 72v–73r), or nos. 121–24 (*Vray dieu, qui me confortera*, fol. 83v; *Vray dieu, qu'amoureux ont de paine*, fol. 84r; *Vray dieu d'amours, confortez-moy*, fols. 84v–85r; *Vray dieu d'amours, reconfortez ma dame*, fols. 85v–86r).[11]

In Petrucci's *Canti C*, fols. 74v–75r, a strict *cantus firmus* four-part arrangement attributed to Crispin de Stappen with the incipit *Gentil galans de gerra* in the superius (arrangement **1c**) presents a variant of the melody in the tenor, transposed up a fourth, first in augmented, then in original values, whereas in another anonymous variant setting within the same book (fols. 14v–15r) (arrangement **1b**) the melody, though still mainly carried by the tenor, also thoroughly pervades the other parts and is freely elaborated, thus striking the ear as more modern in style. Of the two settings, the latter, with its frequent repeated notes, sounds much more vocal in nature and could very well carry the *Paris 12744* text in all of its voices, whereas the de Stappen arrangement has all the features of an instrumental fantasia on a *cantus firmus* tenor. And indeed, almost to confirm this impression, the anonymous version (**1b**) has a full-texted concordance in the later Florentine part-books *Cortona/Paris* (no. 10) and *Florence 164–7* (no. 63). (Example 1 offers the latter's transmission, since *Cortona/Paris* lacks the bassus and also because the former shows on the part of the scribe a slightly more accurate text placement, indirectly betraying a better textual understanding, if not a better orthography). Notable in the anonymous arrangement is the quick alternation, until b. 20, of four duets—1. tenor and bassus; 2. superius and altus; 3. superius and tenor; 4. altus and bassus: only 1. and 2. are separated by a short four-voice interjection, significantly on the verse "*Chi alla guerra allés.*" Each of the duets concludes with a clear-cut cadence corresponding with the end of a verse. It is only starting from b. 20 that the texture changes more consistently to four voices. In this respect it may be interesting to remark how the imitative attack of the second part of Stappen's arrangement seems to allude to mm. 3–5 of the anonymous setting, thus maybe implying a partial compositional filiation (see Example 2).

---

11. But some form of deliberate planning also seems to emerge in ways that are not always so blatant: such is the case of textual and melodical cross-referencing between songs, such as no. 5 "*Sy je suis trouvée/Avecques mon amy*" (fols. 3v–4r) and no. 50 "*Si je suis trouvée/Au boys sur la ramée*" (fol. 34v), both also subtly alluding, though apparently only textually, to the *malmariée* song (whose text is interestingly in Gascogne dialect) "*Se josson mau maridade*" (no. 119, fols. 81v–82r). See Kraft, *Einstimmigkeit um 1500*, 133–42.

Example 1. *Gentil galans de Fransa*, Florence 164–7, no. 63. Variants in Petrucci's *Canti C*, fols. 14v–15r and *Cortona 95–6/Paris 1817* are shown above the corresponding places, with the following abbreviations in italics: *b*=brevis; *sb*=semibrevis; *m*=minima; *sm*=semiminima; *f*=fusa; *d*=dotted. Roman upper and lower case letters following those symbols or in isolation refer to pitches: these have been specified only when strictly necessary or in case the variant concerns just the pitch. An asterisk denotes an error in the concordant source.

Example 1. (*continued*).

Example 1. (*continued*).

Example 1. (*continued*).

Example 1. (*continued*).

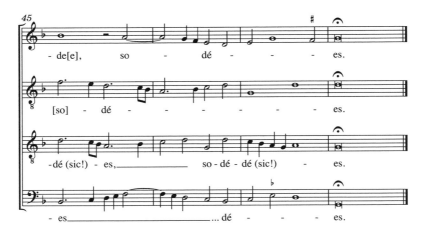

Example 2a. *Gentil galans de Fransa, Florence 164–7*, no. 63, mm. 3–5

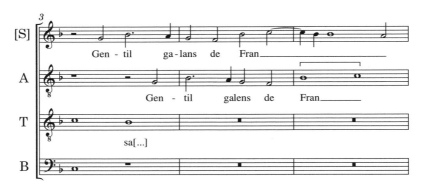

Example 2b. Crispin de Stappen, *Gentil galans de gerra*, Canti C, fols. 74v–75r, mm. 27–29

Example 3a. Crispin de Stappen, *Gentil galans de gerra*, Canti C, fols. 74v–75r, mm. 38–42, showing the hidden parallel octaves.

Example 3b. Prioris, *Gentis galans*, Pernner, pp. 318–19, mm. 38–42, with arrows showing the melodic changes apparently carried out in order to avoid the parallel intervals that occur in the *Canti* C version.

The arrangement attributed in Petrucci to de Stappen is ascribed to Prioris in its only concordance, the later German D-Rp C 120 (*Pernner Codex*), pp. 318–19. Although scholars judge the attribution to Prioris less likely[12] (a fact moreover confirmed by the probable sequence of its transmission, as we shall see below), that source offers a slightly better reading. In a couple of places (mm. 38–39 and 41–42), *Pernner* displays a turn of phrase in, respectively, superius and

---

12. See Litterick, "Prioris, Johannes," and Boorman & Haggh, "Stappen, Crispin"; also Douglas & Keahey, *Johannes Prioris*, XXI–II (commentary) and 121–23 (transcription), and Haggh, "Crispijne and Albertijne," 334.

Example 4a. *Nous n'y porteron plus d'espée, Paris 12744, fol. 96v*

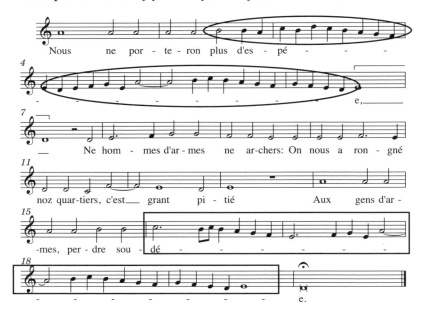

contra, which avoids the hidden parallel perfect intervals cropping up in the *Canti C* concordance. (See Example 3.) That *Pernner* may be related to Petrucci (certainly not unusual for German sources of this period) is suggested moreover by at least a conjunctive error: at m. 47 both *Canti C* and *Pernner* read the third note in the superius as c', which of course patently clashes with the tenor's b-flat.[13] However the different attributions in the two sources would make a direct filiation from Petrucci rather problematic.

The French texts in *Cortona/Paris* and *Florence 164–7* are generally badly misspelled, as is the norm for Italian sources of this period, and the concordances to the anonymous *Canti C* arrangement (**1b**) are no exceptions to this. What is interesting is rather that, beyond the first four lines, forming the first stanza, the poem continues completely differently from its French

---

13. Another possible conjunctive error is the dissonance *b*-flat / *a'* between superius and contra in m. 45. See Douglas & Keahey, *Johannes Prioris*, p. XXII. Birkendorf, *Der Codex Pernner*, attributes the music copied between pages 174 and 341 (thus including the piece in question) to Hand E, whom he judges less indebted, if at all, to *Canti C*'s transmission of Franco-Flemish chansons (vol. 1, 20 and 64–65), though he does admit that "*Gentil galans*" (78), as well as other works (89) may have reached the *Pernner* copyist(s) from Italy. At pp. 254–55 he proposes a phrasal analysis of the melody as appearing in the tenor, also briefly sketching out phrase distribution of the borrowed melody in the other voices.

Example 4b. *Gentil galans de Fransa/Et nous ne porteron plus d'espée*, *Florence 164–7*, mm. 20–26 and mm. 43–49

transmission. As pointed out by Isabel Kraft,[14] the extra lines seem to quote from another song in *Paris 12744*: this is *Nous n'y porteron plus d'espée*, no. 140, fol. 96v. (See Example 4.)

However, if the music quotation is a pretty close and anyhow quite recognizable 'rationalized' version (compare, for instance, the first phrase of the monophonic version, richly embellished and varied in its final reprise as

---

14. See, in this respect, Kraft, *Einstimmigkeit um 1500*, 265.

Example 4b. (*continued*).

opposed to its polyphonic setting, purged of nearly all flourishes and identically repeated at the end), the text's transmission tells a different story, as the synoptic comparison of the texts below shows:

Cortona/Paris, no. 10 and *Florence 164–7,* no. 63

"Gentil galans de Fransa,
Chi alla guerra alés,
Je vous pri chi vo playse
Mon amy salués"
"Et nous ne porteron plus d'espée
Puische le roy nous a casés
Et nous a rogné nos sodées."

Paris 12744*, fol. 96*v
Nous n'y porteron plus d'espée,
Ne hommes d'armes, ne archers:
On nous a rongné noz quartiers.
C'est grant pitié
Aux gens d'armes perdre soudée.
Noz lances s'y sont defferrées,
Noz espées n'ont point de pointe;
Nous pillerons les gens par tout.
C'est grant pitié ...
Nous crirons tous à la vollée:
"Hée, noble roy, vous avez tort.
Vostre feu père, qui est mort,
Ne feist jamais perdre soudée."

The polyphonic version seems to have joined two completely different songs sharing a war-related topic, though within sharply diverging contexts: whereas in *Gentilz gallans de France* the soldiers addressed by the lady merely report on her lover's death (apparently brought about by a fight against the Bretons), *Nous n'y porteron plus d'espée* is a song expressing the warriors' rage at having lost their livelihood ("*on nous a rongné noz quartiers...perdre soudée*")[15] and for this reason threatening to violently unleash their frustration onto the helpless population ("*nous pillerons les gens par tout*"), an event not at all infrequent in mercenaries' armies of the late Middle Ages. If Gaston Paris was right in stating that the praise offered to "*vostre feu père*" who "*ne feist jamais perdre soudée*" (literally "never had [us] lose money,"[16] probably meaning that he never failed to pay his soldiers) in the last stanza of *Nous n'y porteron* refers to Louis XI, then the pillages mentioned in the second one may be a threat or a blackmailing gesture aimed at his son and successor Charles VIII, who more than once found himself unable to remunerate his army: for example, payments to the mercenary Swiss troops stationed in Geneva in the Spring-Summer of 1494 and waiting to be deployed in Italy were already several months in arrears.[17] In addition, letters by Charles to the citizens of Troyes allude to "*pilleries des gens de guerre*" perpetrated in Champagne in June

---

15. In Middle French, *quartier, quarteron,* or *quartonier* (with the variants *cartonier*, etc.) may mean the fourth part of a measure of something, such as food or a piece of land, whereas *rongner* means to trim, cut back. Thus, in this context the phrase may mean "they have cut back our due." *Soudée* or *soldée* has in this context the meaning of "wage," "emoluments." See Godefroy, *Dictionnaire de l'ancienne langue française*.

16. See Gevaert and Paris, *Chansons du XVe siècle*, 143.

17. See Labande-Mailfert, *Charles VIII*, 211–12.

and July of the same year, presumably by troops stationed there, waiting to accompany the king in his Italian campaign.[18] It is of course hard to resist connecting this historical fact with the overt menace relayed by the verse "*nous pillerons les gens par tout*" in the monophonic song.

Strictly speaking, however, the Florentine arrangement does not incorporate the two pre-existing songs on an equal footing, for while music and words of the first stanza of *Gentilz gallans de France* are cited almost literally, the same cannot be said of *Nous n'y porteron plus d'espée*. Indeed, just as the music is a 'rationalized' borrowing of the *Paris 12744* melody—see above—, the three lines of text are a pithy and eloquent summary of the three original stanzas, whereby the accusation against the king who causes the ruin of his soldiers is much more direct and to the point. It might also be added that the verse "*puische le roy nous a casés*" might have ominously brought back memories of the catastrophic defeat of the Medici party indirectly caused by Charles VIII's entry into Florence in 1494, a reference that was quite appropriate for two manuscripts more or less associated with the Medici and their sympathizers and likely compiled during the papacy of Leo X. In this sense one might attribute this 'new' line and the 'condensed' chanson text to the 'Florentine' musician, although this presupposes a good knowledge of the French language on his part, which seems difficult to demonstrate. Undoubtedly, however, the underlay of the text in *Paris 12744* (Example 5) seems to work better than the shortened version found in the Italian sources. In any case, whether the modified text is the work of the composer or of the Italian scribe, the apparently nonsensical juxtaposition of *Gentilz gallans de France* with *Nous n'y porteron plus d'espée* might go beyond a purely musical play, since both texts seem to imply, each in its own, specific context, the French army and King Charles VIII as main actors, presenting them in two critical moments of French history, yet portraying the two different situations from the soldiers' perspective. After all, what the composer does here is not so much different from the earlier 'combinative' song, with the notable difference that in this case the associative play takes place horizontally and successively.

The musical readings of *Canti C*, *Cortona/Paris* and *Florence 164–7* are all very close. The two Florentine sources are nearly contemporary,[19] and may be

---

18. See Lemonnier, *La France sous Charles* VIII, 25–26.

19. For the most likely dating of the two manuscript part books, see, respectively, two studies by Cummings: "Giulio de' Medici's Music Books," 95–97 (ca. 1519–23), and MS *Florence*, 51 (ca. 1518–21).

Example 5. *Gentil galans de Fransa*, mm. 26–48, showing both the text as appearing in the sources, as well as the corresponding text of *Nous n'y porteron plus d'espée* in *Paris 12744*, fol. 96v

Example 5. (*continued*).

Example 5. (*continued*).

still closer related, directly or indirectly linked as they are to the Medici cultural environment.[20] Moreover, ascertaining the degree of codicological kinship between the two manuscripts is complicated by the loss of the bassus part for *Cortona/Paris*: in the case of *Gentil galans* it would have confirmed or not the correct *e*-flat reading in m. 29 of *Florence 164–7* (instead of the evidently erroneous *d* of *Canti C*. (See Example 1, m. 29.) On the other hand, the French misspellings are quite similar, if not always identical (see, for instance, *Fransa* for *France*, *guerra* for *guerre*, *chi* for *qui*) and clearly seem to

---

20. This should not necessarily imply that the several concordances be in a direct stemmatic relationship with each other; indeed in some cases such a relationship is demonstrably not possible. See Cummings, *MS Florence*, 39.

point to Italian scribes either with a very approximate French command or perhaps attempting a phonetic spelling. Interestingly, as Cummings observes,[21] most of the French repertory transmitted in *Florence 164–7* has concordances either in *Cortona/Paris* or in *Strozzi*, but, with few exceptions, not in both,[22] suggesting two different repertorial strains at work in the three sources. Further, *Strozzi* was likely written by a French-speaking scribe for a Florentine patron (one at times even hostile to the Medici party), while *Cortona/Paris* was compiled for a Medici scion by an Italian scribe. Finally, it seems likely that the French repertory common to the latter and *Florence 164–7* had been in circulation for some time in Florence, or at least in Medici circles, as demonstrated by its many concordances with other earlier or contemporary Florentine sources also in one way or another linked to the Tuscan ruling family, whereas the exclusively French music transmitted by *Strozzi* has most of its concordances north of the Alps, with the important exception of Petrucci's *Canti* series. However, if these considerations suggest that most of the French concordances in *Cortona/Paris* and *Florence 164–7* had one or more common ancestors also originating in Florence or in its immediate vicinity, the proposed references in *Gentil galans de Fransa/Et nous ne porteron plus d'espée*, and in the related arrangement by Crispin/Prioris, to specific events linked to Charles VIII's war adventures require us to further investigate the possible context of its first diffusion. But first of all we should look more in detail at the circumstances of its earliest available—textless—transmission in Petrucci.

Textlessness

The *Canti* C reading is of course the earliest source for **1b**, and no previous concordance to this four-part arrangement of the *Paris 12744* chanson has thus far come to light. Since many of the songs found with only a text incipit in the Petrucci *Canti* books have texted concordances in contemporary or slightly earlier French and later Italian chansonniers, it seems likely that this version of *Gentil(z) gal(l)ans de France (gerra)* should also originally have carried a text, one more or less close to the one found in *Cortona/Paris* and *Florence 164–7*.

At first sight it might seem strange that, of the dozens of secular pieces supplied to Petrucci by his editor, Petrus Castellanus, none (except the few

---

21. Ibid. 54.
22. Cummings errs however in thinking Compère's "*Une playsant filette*" is the sole French composition common to the three sources, as shown by the concordance list of *Strozzi* in Brown, "The Music of the Strozzi Chansonnier," 124–26.

liturgical ones) was provided with a full text.[23] Boorman surmises that he may have acquired them as they stand[24] and, as a possible cause for this situation, he mentions ignorance of the French language on the part of most bourgeois music amateurs, whom he assumes to have been the main recipients of the *Canti* series.[25] This may very well be true, since Petrucci's *Frottole* editions (starting in 1504) are indeed provided with full texts, even including additional stanzas for the superius part.[26] It must however be observed that even the few Italian pieces present in the *Canti* are untexted beyond the incipit (the only fully texted pieces being the few Latin, sacred ones) and that this situation, as Boorman himself points out,[27] is not unlike that of several late 15th-century, mainly Florentine, chansonniers, certainly not prepared for bourgeois amateurs and demonstrably owned by either professional musicians or even high-placed officials.[28] If, therefore, Boorman's sociological explanation should in any way constitute an argument for the absence of text, it remains to be explained why basically all Italian chansonniers of the 1480s/90s (possibly with the notable exception of the Florentine F-Pn, f. fr. 15123—the *Pixérécourt Chansonnier*—whose French is, anyway, far from impeccable), certainly not prepared for the general public, are also almost entirely textless prior to about 1515–20, when collections such as the part-books *Florence 164–7* and

---

23. For Castellanus' role as musical editor, see Blackburn, "Petrucci's Venetian Editor" and, in addition (concerning the usage of special mensuration signs), "The Sign of Petrucci's Editor."

24. See Boorman, *Ottaviano Petrucci*, 260. That this may be so is reinforced by the fact that incipits go from just a couple of words (most commonly) up to entire sentences (as, for instance, in *Canti C*, "L'oserai-ge dire se j'ame par amours," no. 30, fols. 45v–46r or even "Mon amy m'avoyt promis une belle chainture," no. 64, fols. 84v–85r). This may well indicate that indeed Castellanus provided as much text as he could, although it should not automatically imply, as will be shown below, that the content or the topic of at least a few songs was unknown to him.

25. See Boorman, *Ottaviano Petrucci*, 270.

26. See ibid., 280. It should be added that the prevailingly syllabic setting—often with several repeated notes—and the close structural adherence of music to text in the frottola would make an untexted transmission almost meaningless. For more on the relationship between literary text and music in the Petrucci frottola prints, see ibid.

27. Ibid., 150.

28. We are here referring, in particular, to three important Florentine chansonniers (I-Fn, MS Magl. XIX, 176, 178 and *Florence 229*) and one from Ferrara (I-Rc MS 2856 [*Casanatense*]). For literature on and editions of these sources, see, respectively, Piette, "Florence, Biblioteca Nazionale Centrale, Magliabechi XIX, 176"; Powers, "The Music Manuscript Fondo Magliabechi XIX.178"; Brown, *A Florentine Chansonnier*; Lockwood, *Music in Renaissance Ferrara*, 226 and 269–71 and, for a facsimile, Lockwood, *A Ferrarese Chansonnier*. A complete transcription with concordances is contained in Wolff, "The Chansonnier Biblioteca Casanatense."

Cortona/Paris, in addition to *Strozzi*, carry for the first time complete texts.[29] However, even in these later sources (with the single exception of the last—whose scribe might in any case have been a Frenchman),[30] the French orthography is so poor and so evidently hampered by frequent Italianisms, that, based alone on their evidence, no direct connection can be established between the ability to understand and pronounce French and a higher social standing and/or professional musicianship in Italy until at least the early 1520s.[31]

---

29. One should also add, of course, that Petrucci's very first editions, such as the *Canti* series, needed to address as many potential customers as possible, most of whom may have had scarce, if at all, knowledge of French.

30. See above. It should not seem surprising to find French scribes working in Italy, assuming, as it seems likely, that *Strozzi* was indeed copied in Florence. Joshua Rifkin supports the French origins of the scribe, particularly in view of his consistent employment of dialect forms in texts, adding, moreover, that the assemblage of the manuscript in quaternions contradicts current Florentine preference for quinternions (see "Referat Brown—Diskussion" at the end of Brown, "Words and Music," 122). Bernstein, "A Florentine Chansonnier," makes a compelling case for a contemporary source, where the contributions of Italian and French scribes can be sharply distinguished by, amongst other things, language and texting conventions.

31. This might seem surprising, in light of the conspicuous Francophile attitude in Florence before and after the Medici, indeed, since at least the later 14th century. See, in this respect, Maissen, "Ein Mythos wird Realität." That the situation must have been entirely different and that French must have been well known amongst the nobility, professional musicians and poets until about 1440, is aptly shown by Fallows, "French as a Courtly Language." It must however be pointed out, as the author also does, that most surviving Italian sources, from the early 15th century, that included French polyphony come from the North of the peninsula, most notably from the Veneto, where a French cultural influence (in part via the Visconti court) must have been more pronounced—whereas many chansonniers written in Italy after about 1440 (for the most part nearly textless, or with a very garbled French as we have seen) were redacted in central Italy (mainly Tuscany and Florence) and, to a minor extent, in the South. Poor or absent knowledge of French on the part of these scribes should not of course be generalized to imply that, after about mid century, the ruling classes had simply and suddenly become incapable in French: otherwise Du Fay would not have written an elaborate letter in this language to Piero and Giovanni de' Medici in 1456 (cf. ibid., 440): nor, a year later, would Galeazzo Maria Sforza have communicated to his father the necessity of entertaining his company by reading aloud in French, implicitly suggesting that he would be better understood than if he read in Latin (ibid., 431 & 441). But of course Galeazzo Maria had spent a couple of years in France in his early youth, and his wife, Bona of Savoy, was French-speaking; moreover Galeazzo's younger brother and future cardinal, Ascanio, had at age fifteen "a steward who could sing French and Italian songs" (see Lowinsky, "Ascanio Sforza's Life," 45), as he himself wrote in a letter to his brother the Duke, a fact which may point to the currency of the French language as a sign of worldly distinction in the Milanese and other North Italian courts of the Renaissance. This was also remarked long ago by Gianfranco Folena, who in "La cultura volgare," 151, noted that "la conoscenza del francese [...] era un segno della nuova classe aristocratica nell'Italia settentrionale." Having said that, one should not forget that the ability to understand and the ability to speak and write correctly in a foreign language are two completely different things. Moreover, the 'nobility' should not be understood as a cohesive social group, being at least as stratified as the 'commoners,' so that not all aristocrats may necessarily have mastered French or other foreign languages at a comparable, reasonably high level. (For this last and the preceding important observation in n29 I wish to thank Stanley Boorman).

Returning to our song, if *gerra* stays for *guerra*, the implication might be that, even if Castellanus did not have the text for this song, he was at least well aware of its war-related content.[32] As Bonnie Blackburn demonstrated a few years ago,[33] Petrus Castellanus, was "certainly not beyond changing the texts he provided to Petrucci."[34] But in her article Blackburn was mainly concerned with changes due to doctrinal or religious questions—moreover, limited to single words—and so she did not specifically tackle textual discrepancies in the incipits of the three *Canti* books. An examination of unique textual deviations, not found in earlier sources (excluding purely orthographic variants and later, sacred contrafacta), has revealed that most of them occur in *Canti C* and that they are prevailingly located in the last section of the book. Table 2 enumerates the pieces according to their position in the editions, and gives the alternative readings in the concordant source or sources (intabulations being excluded from consideration).[35]

Interesting and revealing are the textual changes in *Odhecaton*, no. 49; *Canti B*, no. 46; and *Canti C*, nos. 90 and 91. As regards no. 49 of *Odhecaton*, the incipit, suggesting an instrumental piece, would seem much closer to its musical character rather than the motet-like title of *Segovia*. Very interesting and illuminating is also no. 46 of *Canti B*, which seems to point to an Italian and, in particular, Florentine tradition for the apparently 'odd' incipit, a tradition which obviously includes Castellanus's transmission. On the other hand, whereas both incipits connected with *Canti C*, no. 91 seem to suggest a now lost French court poem, no. 90 has a complete Italian popularizing text in *Colombina*, of which the incipit in *Canti C* may be a garbled recollection. All this seems to confirm that Castellanus or some intermediary was certainly aware of the general meaning of these texts, even if he did not happen to have

---

32. While it is true that in Italian, as in French, "gerra" without the "u" would be spoken with a soft "g," this may just be a case of not so infrequent misspelling. One could of course also interpret "de" as indicating provenance, in which case "gerra" may designate a locality. To my knowledge, the only town in this period which could have been mispronounced as "Gerre" or "Gerra" by native Italians is Ger, which is located in western Normandy, nowadays Département Manche. In fact Ger is not too far from the borders of late 15th-century Brittany, the region referred to in the song and one might be tempted to speculate that the *Gentilz gallans* hailed from this town. There is however nothing in the song to suggest this, and it is difficult to imagine that Castellanus or his associates in Venice might have had access to such 'remote' information.

33. Cf. Blackburn, "Petrucci's Venetian Editor," 15–45.

34. Personal communication.

35. The concordances mainly rely on Boorman, *Ottaviano Petrucci*.

Table 2. *Gentilz gallans* songs acording to their position in the editions with alternate readings in concordant sources.

Odhecaton
49. *La stangetta** (Werbech), fols. 54v–55r = *Ortus de celo flos est* (incipit) (Ysac) in E-SE s.s. (*Segovia Codex*), fol. 172r = *Ce n'est pas moy* (full text) in I-Bc MS Q.16 (*Bologna Q.16*), fols. 68v–69r.
66. *Madame, hélas*, fols. 71v–72r = (textless) in E-Sco 5-I-43 (*Colombina Chansonnier*), fols. 124v–125r and I-VEcap MS DCCLVII, fols. 7v–8r = *Dux Carlus* (title; otherwise textless) in Bologna Q.16, fols. 145v–146r.

Canti B
44. *Adieu fillette de regnon*, fols. 48v–49r = *Sol re ut re ut* (title; otherwise textless) in D-B MS Mus. 40021, fol. 30v = (textless) in S-U Vokalmusik i Handskrift 76a (Ysac), fols. 67v–68r.
46. *Je vous emprie* (Agricola), fols. 50v–51r = *Je vous vous en* (incipit) (Alexander) in Florence 178, fols. 23v–24r and *Je vous* (incipit) in *Florence 229*, fols. 275v–277r = *Se vous voulez* (incipit) in F-Pn, f. fr. 1597, fols. 17v–19r, GB-Lbl, Royal 20.A.xvi (incipit) fols. 5v–7r and I-Fr Ms. 2794 (Agricola), fols. 30v–31r.

Canti C
9. *Gentil galant de gerra*, fols. 14v–15r = *Gentil galans de France* (full text) in *Cortona / Paris*, no. 10 and *Florence 164–7* (full text) no. 63. This, together with *Gentil galans de gerra*, fols. 74v–75r, is based on the monophonic melody *Gentilz gallans de France* (full text) in *Paris 12744*, fol. 87v.
80. *Je suy d'Alemagne / Joliettement m'en vay*, fols. 106v–107r = *Je suis dalle magne* (i.e., without the second text) (full text in superius; incipit in all other voices) in *Florence 229*, fols. 168v–170r.
89. *Très doulx regart* = textless in the only other known source, *Florence 229*, fols. iiiiv–1r (Jannes Martini).
90. *Questa se chiama*, fols. 115v–116r (Jo. Japart) = *Famene un pocho di quella mazacrocha* (full text) in *Colombina*, fols. 128v–129r.
91. *Serviteur soye*, fols. 116v–117r (Jo. Sthokem) = *Hellas dame* (incipit) in *Florence 229*, fols. 159v–160r.
135. *Vous dont fortune*, fols. 163v–164r = *La mi lares vous dont* (incipit) in *Casanatense*, fols. 134v–136r (Jo. Ghiselin).

* For the possible connection of this piece to Marchesino Stanga, Ludovico Sforzas 'tesoriere' and personal counsellor, see Kämper. "La stangetta."

them available. In that case the epithet *de gerra* for the *Canti* transmission of **1b** and **1c**, both based on **1a**, might have served to clearly distinguish them from *Gentil galant aventuriers* (**2b**) on fols. 43v–44r, also based on another song transmitted in *Paris 12744*.[36] Needless to say, this indirectly points to a diffusion of the song in Italian circles prior to its being included in Petrucci's print.

---

36. In at least another case of homonymy Petrucci distinguishes the two items by adding an 'ad hoc' descriptive complement to the title: the *Missa L'homme armé sexti toni* as opposed to *L'homme armé super voces musicales* in *Misse Josquin* (1502): see Blackburn, "Masses Based on Popular Songs," 68, n38.

Another Song by Compère?

As already mentioned, arrangement **1b** is anonymous in all three concordant sources. In *Canti C* it is preceded by another anonymous piece, a setting of O *Venus bant*, and followed by la Rue's *Myn hert*; in *Cortona/Paris* it is preceded and followed by compositions attributed elsewhere to Compère; and in *Florence 164–7* it is preceded by an anonymous combinative chanson and followed, again, by a four-part arrangement ascribed in other sources to Compère. Interestingly the Compère chanson (*Je suis amie du forrier*) which, in *Cortona/Paris*, precedes *Gentil galans de Fransa*, follows it in *Florence 164–7*.[37] Compère is a composer known for having set several four-part arrangements of pre-existing 'popularizing' melodies, being also on the whole one of the best represented in Petrucci's *Canti* series, though in fact often without attribution. It is therefore not impossible that *Gentil galans* may also be by the French composer—and there is support for such an ascription in its stylistic features: terse contrapuntal discourse, with the monophonic model being mainly quoted in superius and tenor, though also freely migrating to the other voices; frequent exchanges of motives between the parts; phrasal articulation that is respectful of the 'borrowed' melody's layout; a full texture alternating with sprightly duets; and the bassus often moving from V to I degree at cadences.[38] Furthermore there are two other compositions, demonstrably by Compère, in which the same independent song, ostensibly also based on a *cantus prius factus*, is seamlessly attached as a second part.[39]

After his Milanese years in the early 1470's, Compère is documented as *chantre ordinaire* to Charles VIII (1486), additionally becoming singer in the royal chapel in 1494.[40] Although "[i]t is not certain that the royal chapel accompanied the king," the composer was a member of Charles's entourage during his Italian expedition,[41] implying that he must have travelled for just

---

37. Authorship is drawn from *Capp. Giulia*, since all compositions in the two Florentine manuscripts are anonymous.

38. For this last trait, see also Zuckerman Wesner, "The Chansons of Loyset Compère," 498.

39. These are "*Alon fère nos barbes*" and "*Mon père m'a donné mari*," both of which are joined without interruption to the obscene song "*Et où la trouveroye/La femme au petit con.*" It might be a humorous coincidence, but the second line of "*Alon fère nos barbes*" also mentions some "*gentil galans*," albeit of an entirely different nature than the military protagonists of "*Gentilz gallans de France*! For a modern transcription and a list of concordances, see Finscher, *Loyset Compère*, 5, 1972, respectively at 8–9 and 38–40.

40. For this information see Rifkin et al., "Compère, Loyset."

41. See Sherr, *Papal Music Manuscripts*, 16, and Lockwood, "Music at Ferrara in the Period of Ercole I d'Este," 115–16 and 129–30.

less than a year during 1494 and 1495, throughout the Italian peninsula, maybe even sojourning, if only briefly, in Florence (subdued by the king at the end of 1494), in addition of course to Rome (basically occupied by the king's forces in January 1495) and Naples, where the king and his retinue stayed for about three months, from March until May. Charles' passage through Florence was certainly too short and, above all, too late to explain the not insignificant place that Compère's compositions had already occupied in Florentine chansonniers since the early 1490s[42]—but the approximately one-month long Roman stay in January 1495 would certainly have provided the composer with ample opportunities to come into contact with local musicians, notably singers of the papal chapel, especially considering that Charles heard mass every day.[43] And, most importantly, if (as it seems) his stay in the papal capital left a trace in the five motets and a Magnificat setting all copied around 1495–7 in V-CVbav, MS Capp. Sist. 15,[44] he should also have had enough time and leisure to compose a chanson based on two war-related melodies perhaps sung by the soldiers, which subsequently might have found its way into Italian sources. Although it is actually more likely that he heard or knew the monophonic songs in the North and composed his setting there, bringing it along with him to Italy, yet, in the case of *Gentilz gallans de France/Nous n'y porteron plus d'espée*, the 'French' Loyset Compère[45] might be a very good candidate for the specific conduit of two such distinctly French songs carrying such unambiguous references (at least for a French audience) to local historical events. Incidentally, placing the composition around 1495 tallies quite nicely with Finscher's suggestion that most of the four-part songs must have been written shortly before 1501–5, that is not many years before their inclusion in their earliest sources, including Petrucci's editions.[46] For all of these reasons, it seems plausible that this arrangement of *Gentilz gallans de France* could also be by Compère.

---

42. For example, *Florence 229*, which, according to Brown, must have been copied between 1490 and 1491 or, according to Rifkin, between 1492 and 1493. See Brown, *A Florentine Chansonnier*, text vol., 25–47 and Rifkin, "Pietrequin Bonnel," 284–96. Rifkin's dating (at ibid., 295, n33) is based on a surmised biographical circumstance for Pietrequin's "*Adieu Florens la jolye*" (fols. 150v–151r) and the fact that the composer left Florence in the Spring of 1493.

43. See Sherr, *Papal Music Manuscripts*, 16.

44. See ibid. and Rifkin et al., "Compère, Loyset."

45. Although Compère—technically a subject of the Empire, having been born in Hainaut—was only naturalized French by Charles VIII in 1494, he had by then already long been associated with French royal circles and, consequently, its culture and musical repertory.

46. See Finscher, *Loyset Compère*, 240.

While the appearance of the chanson in the late Florentine anthologies *Cortona/Paris* and *Florence 164–7*, likely compiled during the papacy of Leo X and the former directly, the latter indirectly linked to the Medici,[47] might be easily explained as an indirect product of the intense cultural relationships entertained between the Francophile Medici pope and his hometown, its first known appearance, in *Canti C*, would be more difficult to clarify. However, if, as Blackburn has shown,[48] Castellanus' alleged good contacts in Rome—and his probable association with the dedicatee and patron or prospective patron of *Odhecaton*, the well-travelled and well-connected Venetian ambassador, the distinguished humanist Girolamo Donato or Donà, also resident in Rome for several periods of time[49]—may have allowed him to get hold of at least some of the sacred repertoire later printed in the Petrucci mass and motet anthologies, it is not at all unthinkable that the Roman channel could also have been available for some secular pieces by composers whose residence in the papal city would have allowed their songs to circulate there. Moreover, we know that Donato was also interested in secular music, from a letter written by Lorenzo de' Medici to his ambassador in Rome, Pietro Alamanni, where he announces he will soon send the *canti* that Donato, then the Venetian colleague to Alamanni in Rome, had requested of him.[50] In this connection, the *cantus firmus* arrangement by Crispin de Stappen of *Gentilz gallans de France* even reinforces the theory of a Roman transmission, since the composer was a singer in the papal chapel almost uninterruptedly from 1493 until 1507 and he may also

---

47. See Cummings, "Giulio de' Medici's Music Books" and *MS Florence*, in particular 42–44, 47–49, and 51–52.

48. See Blackburn, "Petrucci's Venetian Editor," 28–30, although Boorman cannot see a direct Roman connection before 1515/16. See *Ottaviano Petrucci*, 311 and 313.

49. Donato served in Rome between 1491 and 1492, and, most notably for our concerns, between 1497 and 1499, then again in 1505 and from 1509 until his death in 1511. For a succinct overview of his diplomatic and literary career, see Rigo, "Donà, Girolamo" and, in addition, Blackburn, "Lorenzo de' Medici" and "Petrucci's Venetian Editor," 31.

50. See Blackburn, "Lorenzo de' Medici," 19–20. Add to that the fact that a dedicatory letter in a collection of songs, such as *Odhecaton*, would be meaningless had the dedicatee, Donato, shown no interest in secular music. In her article, Blackburn interestingly conjectures that Donato may have reciprocated Petrucci's plea for patronage with music, indirectly suggesting that he was in the possession of at least some of the material which was to flow into the *Canti* series: see ibid., 41.

well have heard the song intoned by, say, the French troops in Rome.[51] It may be worth adding here that Petrucci's preceding secular anthology, *Canti B* (1502), transmits a four-voice arrangement of another political song (*Réveillez-vous, Piccars et Bourguignons*) handed down monophonically in *Paris 12744*, fol. 95r, and also somehow related to Charles, albeit this time much more indirectly and in any case to a period when he was still *dauphin*:[52] could it not be that the passage of Charles and of at least some of his musical retinue in Italy accounts for the transmission also of this song in the Petrucci volume?

'Noble Gallants' in the Church

The fortunes of this melody seem to spill over into the liturgical realm as well, for a *Missa Gentils gallans de France* opens the Roman manuscript *Capp. Sist. 41*, apparently compiled between ca. 1482 and 1507, though for the most part after ca. 1497.[53] In this unique transmission, the mass (which unfortunately lacks the superius and tenor of the first *Kyrie* and *Christe*, due to the loss of fol. 1) is ascribed to "Pintelli," a composer otherwise only known for an Italian ballata.[54] As shown by D'Accone's archival research,[55] a Johannes Pintelli had been active as a singer in Siena Cathedral between 1481 and 1484 and, from 1484 until 1491, in various Florentine church institutions. The presence of his mass in a Roman source is explained by the fact that he ended his career as a member of the papal chapel, where he is recorded from July 1504 and

---

51. Boorman and Haggh, "Stappen, Crispin," supposes the "*Gentils gallans*" arrangement to have originated in Paris, before the composer left his employment at the Sainte Chapelle in 1492, drawing on the unequivocal political and historical associations of the borrowed melody. If it indeed originated in France, it might seem odd to find it uniquely transmitted in *Canti C*, moreover with the melody at the same pitch and identical to the other *Canti C* and Italian variants and *unlike* the slightly different variant transmitted in *Paris 12744*. Further, Rainer Birkendorf's statement that this, along with other songs, may have reached *Pernner* from Italy (see Birkendorf, *Der Codex Pernner*, 89 and n13 above) corroborates the hypothesis of an Italian origin for this "*Gentilz gallans*" setting, too.

52. See Kraft, *Einstimmigkeit um 1500*, CD.

53. Dates taken from http://www.diamm.ac.uk, accessed on 07/28/2013, and Sherr, *Papal Music Manuscripts*, 145–56.

54. See Sherr, "Pintelli, Johannes." The *ballata* "*Questo mostrarsi adirata di fore*" is attributed to Angelo Poliziano in GB-Lbl, Add. MS 16439: see Luisi, "Ben venga maggio," 202; D'Accone, "Some Neglected Composers," 274.

55. See, in particular, the following studies by D'Accone, *The Civic Muse*, 229–30, 234, 254; "Some Neglected Composers"; and "The Singers of San Giovanni," 336–37, 341–42 and 344–46.

where he died shortly before 26 May 1505.[56] His Italian sounding name must have been a local variant, since his engagement record at Santo Spirito in Florence, dated 19 February 1488, unequivocally enters him as "*Giovanni Pintelli francioso*,"[57] while in later Vatican documents he "is consistently called a cleric of the diocese of Avignon."[58]

For several reasons, Pintelli cannot have borrowed the melodic material of *Gentilz gallans de France* from *Canti C*. First of all Petrucci's *Canti* books should never be regarded as the very first source for the music transmitted, but, rather, as collections of music which had already been circulating in manuscript form—and which consequently might have had a chance to sell better—even though *Canti C* does contain a more up-to-date repertory than the previous two anthologies. But, most significantly, Johannes Orceau, the main papal scribe between ca. 1495 until 1512, seems to have copied the mass in Capp. Sist. 41 between ca. 1497 and 1503[59] (possibly even around 1495, if our theory of the Roman transmission of this melody in Italy holds true), but in any case *before* Petrucci issued his anthology, which indirectly makes the Sistine manuscript the first witness for a polyphonic arrangement of *Gentilz gallans de France*, maybe even earlier than its monophonic transmission in *Paris 12744*.

Interestingly the mass is based on two different and independent *Gentil(z) gal(l)ans* melodies and their settings. Indeed, whereas melody **1a** and setting **1b** are the source material for *Kyrie, Gloria, Credo, Osanna* and *Agnus*, *Sanctus* and *Benedictus* are built on arrangement **4a**, which is transmitted in Florentine sources copied in the early 1490s. By contrast, as we know, the Florentine transmission of the music employed in the other movements, found in *Cortona/Paris* and *Florence 164–7*, is a late one, in part possibly even fostered by the intense cultural exchanges between Rome and Florence during the papacy of Leo X, as already suggested.[60] Therefore, the *Sanctus* (but

---

56. See Sherr, "Pintelli, Johannes."

57. See D'Accone, "Some Neglected Composers," 276.

58. See Sherr, "Pintelli." Admittedly the Provençal city (which remained an integral part of the Pope's See until the French Revolution) had been home to many an Italian clerk and appointee of the local papal curia since at least the time of Petrarch; but Pintelli is merely called a "cleric of the diocese," as well as "French."

59. See Sherr, *Papal Music Manuscripts*, 145. Interestingly Orceau was born near the French South-West borders with Brittany, which, in view of the insertion of the initial words of the song in the first *Agnus Dei* (see below) might signal his familiarity with this Breton related melody.

60. But, admittedly, this fact alone cannot rule out that at least some of the music in the two part-book collections pre-dated their compilation by some years.

without the present *Osanna!*) and *Benedictus* could have been composed in the late 1480s, while Pintelli was in Florence, where arrangement **4** was certainly known, whereas the other movements, based on **1a** and **1b**, might have originated later or, in any case, independently. D'Accone argued that "Pintelli drew on these materials because they were current in Florence at the time he was there."[61] However, due to the transmission patterns just delineated, this might only apply for arrangement **4a**.

Although Johannes Pintelli's first recorded entry as a papal singer is for July 1504, this is only a *terminus post quem*, so that it is probable that he might well have already been employed in the Sistine Chapel for a few years before then, even though any records of him between his last Florentine appointment in 1491 and the first known entry of his name in the papal registers in 1504 are lacking. Interestingly, in this respect, D'Accone surmises that the contratenor cited only as "Johannes" in the registers of the papal chapel from March to June 1495 might well be our composer, even speculating that he might have joined the papal chapel immediately or soon after leaving Florence early in 1491.[62] If this is true, then the probability that he composed his mass around 1495, during or after Charles VIII's Roman sojourn, would be much greater and would indirectly support our hypothesis of the Roman origin or at least early diffusion of arrangements **1b** and **1c**, whereas the integration of the arrangement **4a** might just be a memory of his Florentine years, though, as tentatively suggested above, one could hypothesise that *Sanctus* and *Benedictus* were pre-existent—maybe as part of another mass now lost—and that they were incorporated by either the composer or the scribe into the Cappella Sistina mass.[63]

---

61. See D'Accone, "Some Neglected Composers," 277.

62. See D'Accone, *The Civic Muse*, 230, n31 and Sherr, "Pintelli, Johannes." The author gathers the information on the contratenor "Johannes" from Reynolds, *Papal Patronage*, 333. Since papal records from shortly earlier are now lost, it is difficult to say whether Pintelli had already arrived some time earlier (which is possible), and equally whether he stayed continuously up until his certain record in 1504 (which would be highly likely, if the contratenor "Johannes" really should be identical with our composer).

63. *Capp. Sist. 41* contains another mass that has recently been linked to a very specific Roman celebration of 1495: this is Josquin's *Missa La sol fa re mi* (for details see Stewart, "Josquin Desprez" in Macey, et al., "Josquin (Lebloitte dit) des Prez," the author basing himself on hypotheses formulated by Kiang, "Josquin Desprez"). Whether this might help to further circumscribe the dating of the *Missa Gentilz gallans de France* should however remain open, not least in view of the fact that between Pintelli's and Josquin's masses, are placed two *L'homme armé* mass settings by, respectively, Mattheus Pipelare and, again, Josquin. This grouping might conceal a theme of some sort.

Example 6a. Pintelli, *Missa Gentilz gallans de France*, Credo, mm. 43–48

The *Missa Gentilz gallans* displays features both of a *cantus firmus* and of an imitation mass. In fact, particularly in the *Credo*, the composer starts evoking the initial duets of arrangement **1b**, though with different pairs of voices and in slightly staggered fashion. More notably, however, he 'parodies' almost literally the second verse (*Credo*: mm. 7–8; chanson: mm. 6–7) and the beginning of the second part. (See Example 6a–b: *Credo*: mm. 43–48; chanson: mm. 20–26, which is repeated twice more on v. 6) of the song.

Strict *cantus firmus* treatment of **1a** occurs only in the *Osanna* and *Agnus Dei* I. In *Agnus Dei* I the melody is presented on the one hand at the same pitch (*D*) as **1a** and, on the other, in the same 'rationalized' form and with the similar augmented values found in **1c**.[64] The surprise effect is heightened since

---

64. See above and D'Accone, "Some Neglected Composers," 277.

Example 6b. *Gentil galans de Fransa/Nous ne porteron plus d'espée*, mm. 20–26

the bassus actually enters in imitation at a fourth below the tenor, which starts presenting the melody on G—as in the rest of the mass and in the polyphonic transmission in general—only to abandon the exposition in the middle of the second phrase. But that the 'real' presentation of the melody takes place in the lowest voice is made even clearer by the fact that the first phrase in the bassus actually carries the first line of the French text (*Gentilz gallans de France*) exactly underlaid and arranged between the words *Agnus Dei*, placed as an *incipit* under the initial seven breve rests, and the remaining *ordinarium* text (" … *qui tollis peccata mundi* …"). (See Figure 1.)

But the real surprise comes with *Sanctus* and *Benedictus*, thematically unrelated to the other movements, linked as they are to arrangement **4a**, with

Figure 1. Pintelli, *Missa Gentilz gallans de France*, *Agnus Dei I*, Bassus. *Capp. Sist. 41*, fol. 13r. Courtesy Biblioteca Apostolica Vaticana.

which they share mode and some thematic material (see Table 1, above)[65]: compare, for instance, the almost identical passages in mm. 3–5 (*Gentil galans*) and mm. 9–11 (*Sanctus*) (in Example 7a–b) in addition to the altus part at the beginning of the *Sanctus* (mm. 1–4), which is nearly identical to the same part in the chanson at mm. 16–20. (See Example 8a–b.) Most of the time, however, the degree of relationship rests solely on the liberal employment of variations of the same 'tune,' which, in the song, is presented most cogently in the tenor part (Example 9) and which consists of little more than the varied presentation of the 1st species tetrachord on *D* and *G*, both ascending and descending. Yet one may legitimately wonder, whether it makes any sense here to surmise the existence of an independent, pre-existent melody; in fact, even the two *Florence 229* settings share no more than the fourth in question and are based, moreover, on two completely different G modalities: plagal G-tetrardus for the three-voice chanson attributed to Agricola, and authentic G-protus (i.e. with a *b*-flat key signature, notably in <u>all</u> voices) for the four-voice

---

65. Brown, *A Florentine Chansonnier*, text volume, 261 claims that the *Sanctus* and *Benedictus* of the mass are related to 'both' **4a** and **4b**, though clearly the relationship is much stronger with the former. In a personal communication, Bonnie Blackburn pointed out "that the Pintelli mass often lops off the first note of the c.f., which gives more prominence to the descending fourth."

Example 7a. *Gentil galans,* Florence 229, fols. 186v–187r, mm. 1–5

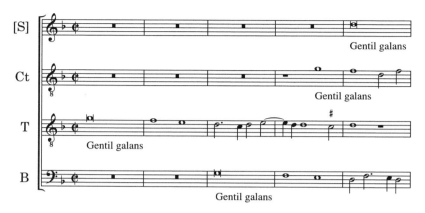

Example 7b. Pintelli, *Missa Gentilz gallans de France,* Sanctus, mm. 9–12

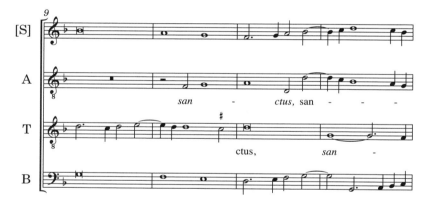

piece. In a way the two *Florence 229* arrangements suggest themselves as instrumental fantasias on a fourth, the common title (in fact little more than a tag) further warranting their relationship. Besides, Agricola's known penchant for composing arrangements on pre-existing polyphonic songs further bolsters the relationship of the two compositions, also indirectly suggesting the chronological priority of the four-voice setting.

At this point, it would be tempting to attribute the arrangement **4a** to Pintelli, given the notable thematic kinship with the *Sanctus* of the mass. In this case, Agricola would have known the arrangement some time after its composition, for, by the time he joined the Cathedral Choir in October 1491,

Example 8a. *Gentil galans*, Florence 229, fols. 186v–187r, mm. 16–20

Example 8b. Pintelli, *Missa Gentilz gallans de France*, Sanctus, mm. 1–4

Pintelli had probably already gone.[66] But equally not implausible is an ascription to Henricus Isaac, who was still in Florence at the time and who, as a singer of S. Giovanni, occasionally also served at the Cathedral. Indeed the pervasive, structural use of a small motive may remind one of 'instrumental' pieces, such as *La Martinella* or *La Morra*, though without the latter's extensive sequences.[67] On the other hand, if one were more inclined to accept Pintelli

---

66. Cf. Wegman, et al. "Agricola [Ackerman], Alexander"; and Sherr, "Pintelli, Johannes."
67. See Strohm and Kempson, "Isaac, Henricus."

Example 9. Tenor of *Gentil galans*, no. 4, *Florence 229*, fols. 186v–187r

as its composer, the reader may wonder why the Frenchman couldn't also have composed the *Gentilz gallans de France/de gerra* setting, thereby making any Compère hypothesis redundant: after all, the exclusively Florentine transmission of the texted concordances in *Cortona/Paris* and *Florence 164–7* might seem natural for a composer who had spent the decisive years of his musical and ecclesiastical career in Florence. However, the arrangements of 'melodies' 1 and 4 are stylistically miles apart and nothing in them points to the same composer, or even the same compositional environment: i.e., hypothetical authorship of one can in no way indirectly support the same for the other. Moreover, apart from the mass and the Italian three-voice ballata—a piece that, if at all, testifies to Pintelli's familiarity with late 15th-century Italian polyphonic traditions, with its prevailingly homorhythmic, vertically directed motion—, nothing else is attributed to this otherwise elusive composer, so that any evaluation based on style alone would basically be very problematic.[68] But it is, of course, plausible that Pintelli might have used the monophonic songs he may have heard hummed or sung by the French soldiers stationed in Rome in 1495 for a four-voice arrangement, thus postulating a purely 'oral' transmission of the two melodies in Italy, a case, by the way, we have also hypothesised in relation to Crispin's composition. Alternatively, the four-voice setting had been arranged, as proposed earlier, by Loyset Compère, a composer already known to Italian musical circles since at least his years at the Sforza court in Milan in the 1470s and who, as we mentioned, visited the Italian peninsula again, as part of Charles VIII's retinue, in 1494–95; interestingly it is shortly thereafter that the composer's first attempts at the 'new' popularizing song type—of which *Gentilz gallans de France/Nous n'y porteron plus d'espée* is a very peculiar example—have been dated. Either way, it seems likely that oral transmission must have played a big part in the circulation of these two melodies, as indeed of others—like the aforementioned *Réveillez-vous, Piccars et Bourguignons*,— which later, thanks to polyphonic arrangements, found their way into anthologies such as Petrucci's *Canti* series. The intriguing thing about the small family of compositions around *Gentilz gallans de France*, is that we may have caught a very specific cultural transfer process indirectly caused by the French occupation of Rome. If this is so, then the French soldiers might have been responsible for other types of transmission, as well as that of syphilis throughout Europe after their hasty return to France later in 1495.

---

68. But one should not forget that Isaac adopted a decisive 'Italianate' style when contributing to the local Florentine tradition in the late 1480s and early 1490s. See ibid.

SOURCES CITED

Manuscripts

RISM siglum	*Abbreviation used in this paper*
B-Br, 228	
D-Rp, C 120	*Pernner*
E-Sc, 5–1–43	*Colombina*
E-SG, s.s.	
F-Pn, f.fr. 9346	*Bayeux*
F-Pn, f.fr. 12744	*Paris 12744*
F-Pn, f.fr. 15123	*Pixérécourt*
F-Pn, nouv. acq. fr. 1817	*Cortona/Paris*
GB-Lbl, Add.MS. 16439	
I-CTb, 95–6	*Cortona/Paris*
I-Fc, Basevi 2439	
I-Fc, Basevi 2442	*Strozzi*
I-Fn, Banco rari 229	*Florence 229*
I-Fn, Magl.XIX, 164–7	*Florence 164–7*
I-Fn, Magl.XIX, 176	
I-Fn, Magl.XIX, 178	*Florence 178*
I-Rc, 2856	*Casanatense*
V-CVbav, Capp.Sist. 15	
V-CVbav, Capp.Sist. 41	*Capp.Sist.41*
V-CVbav, Capp. Giulia XIII, 27	*Capp. Giulia*

Printed Editions

Canti B (Venice: Petrucci, 1502, 1503)
Canti C (Venice: Petrucci, 1504)
Harmonice Musices Odhecaton A (Venice; Petrucci, 1501, 1503, 1504)

Secondary Literature

Atlas, Allan W. *The Cappella Giulia Chansonnier (Rome, Biblioteca Apostolica Vaticana, C. G. XIII. 27), Part 1 (Commentary); Part 2 (Transcriptions).* Wissenschaftliche Abhandlungen 27/1; Musicological Studies 27/1). Brooklyn, NY: Institute of Mediæval Music, 1975.

Bernstein, Lawrence F. "A Florentine Chansonnier of the Early Sixteenth Century: Florence, Biblioteca Nazionale Centrale, MS Magliabechi xix 117." *Early Music History* 6 (1986), 1–107.

Birkendorf, Rainer. *Der Codex Pernner. Quellenkundliche Studien zu einer Musikhandschrift des frühen 16. Jahrhunderts (Regensburg, Bischöfliche Zentralbibliothek, Sammlung Proske, Ms. C 120)*. Collectanea musicologica 6/I–III. Augsburg: Bernd Wißner, 1994.

Blackburn, Bonnie J. "Lorenzo de' Medici, a Lost Isaac Manuscript, and the Venetian Ambassador." In *Musica Franca: Essays in Honor of Frank A. D'Accone,* edited by Irene Alm, Alyson McLamon & Colleen Reardon, 19–44. Festschrift Series 18. Stuyvesant, NY: Pendragon Press, 1996. Reprinted as chapter V in Blackburn, *Composition, Printing and Performance*. Variorum Collected Studies Series; Studies in Renaissance Music. Aldershot and Burlington, VT: Ashgate, 2000.)

———."Masses Based on Popular Songs and Solmization Syllables." In *The Josquin Companion,* edited by Richard Sherr, 51–88. Oxford: Oxford University Press, 2001.

———."Petrucci's Venetian Editor: Petrus Castellanus and His Musical Garden." *Musica Disciplina* 49 (1995), 15–45. Reprinted as chapter VI in Blackburn, *Composition, Printing and Performance*.

———. "The Sign of Petrucci's Editor." In *Venezia 1501: Petrucci e la stampa musicale / Venice 1501: Petrucci, Music, Print and Publishing: Atti del Convegno Internazionale di Studi. Venezia—Palazzo Giustinian Lolin, 10–13 ottobre 2001,* edited by Giulio Cattin & Patrizia Dalla Vecchia, 415–29. Venice: Edizioni Fondazione Levi, 2005.

Boorman, Stanley. *Ottaviano Petrucci: A Catalogue Raisonné*. Oxford: Oxford University Press, 2006.

———, & Barbara H. Haggh. "Stappen, Crispin [Crispiaenen, Crispijn] van [van der, de]." In: *Grove Music Online* (http://www.oxfordmusiconline.com), accessed on 03/17/2014.

Brown, Howard M. *A Florentine Chansonnier from the Time of Lorenzo the Magnificent: Florence, Biblioteca Nazionale Centrale, MS B R 229*. Monuments of Renaissance Music 7. Chicago & London: University of Chicago Press, 1983.

———."The Chanson rustique: Popular Elements in the 15th- and 16th-Century Chanson." *Journal of the American Musicological Society* 12 (1959), 16–26.

———. "The Music of the Strozzi Chansonnier (Florence, Biblioteca del Conservatorio di Musica, MS Basevi 2442)." *Acta Musicologica* 40 (1968), 115–29.

———. "The Transformation of the Chanson at the End of the Fifteenth Century." In *Report of the Tenth Congress of the International Musicological Society,* Ljubljana 1967, edited by Dragotin Cvetko, 78–94. Kassel: Bärenreiter, 1970.

———. "Words and Music in Early 16th-Century Chansons: Text Underlay in Florence, Biblioteca del Conservatorio, Ms Basevi 2442." In *Formen und Probleme der Überlieferung mehrstimmiger Musik im Zeitalter Josquins Desprez*, edited by Ludwig Finscher, 97–141. Wolfenbütteler Forschungen 6; Quellenstudien zur Musik der Renaissance 1. Munich: Kraus International Publications, 1981.

Bulst, Neithard. "Karl VIII. 1483–1498." In *Die französischen Könige des Mittelalters. Von Odo bis Karl VIII. 888–1498*, edited by Joachim Ehlers, Heribert Müller & Bernd Scheidmüller, 331–49. Munich: Verlag C. H. Beck, 2006/2.

Cummings, Anthony M. "Giulio de' Medici's Music Books." *Early Music History* 10 (1991), 65–122.

———. *MS Florence, Biblioteca Nazionale Centrale, Magl. XIX, 164–167*. Royal Musical Association Monographs 15. Aldershot and Burlington, VT: Ashgate, 2006.

D'Accone, Frank A. "Some Neglected Composers in the Florentine Chapels, Ca. 1475–1525." *Viator. Medieval and Renaissance Studies* 1 (1970), 263–88.

———. *The Civic Muse: Music and Musicians in Siena during the Middle Ages and the Renaissance*. Chicago: University of Chicago Press, 1997.

———. "The Singers of San Giovanni in Florence during the Fifteenth Century." *Journal of the American Musicological Society* 14 (1961), 307–58.

Fallows, David. *A Catalogue of Polyphonic Songs, 1415–1480*. Oxford: Oxford University Press, 1999.

———. "French as a Courtly Language in Fifteenth-Century Italy: The Musical Evidence." *Renaissance Studies* 3 (1989), 429–41. Reprinted as chapter VI in Fallows, *Songs and Musicians in the Fifteenth Century*. Collected Studies Series. Aldershot: Variorum, 1996.

Finscher, Ludwig. *Loyset Compère (c. 1450–1518): Life and Works*. Musicological Studies and Documents 12. s.l.: American Institute of Musicology, 1964.

———, editor. *Loyset Compère: Opera omnia*. Corpus Mensurabilis Musicae 15. Rome: American Institute of Musicology, 1958–72.

Folena, Gianfranco. "La cultura volgare e l'Umanesimo cavalleresco nel Veneto." In *Umanesimo europeo e Umanesimo veneziano*, edited by Vittore Branca, 141–59. Florence: Sansoni, 1963.

Gérold, Théodore. *Le Manuscrit de Bayeux: texte et musique d'un recueil de chansons du XVe siècle*. Strasbourg: Commission des Publications de la Faculté de Lettres, Palais de l'Université, 1921.

Godefroy, Frédéric. *Dictionnaire de l'ancienne langue française*. Online under http://micmap.org/dicfro/next/dictionaire-godefroy/447/7/sold%C3%A9e, accessed on 09/29/2014.

Haggh, Barbara H. "Crispijne and Albertijne: Two Tenors at the Church of St Niklaas, Brussels." *Music & Letters* 76 (1995), 325–44.

Kämper, Dietrich. "La staéngetta—eine Instrumentalkomposition Gaspars van Weerbeke?" In *Ars musica musica scientia: Festschrift Heinrich Hüschen zum fünfundsechzigsten Geburtstag am 2. März 1980*, edited by Detlef Altenburg, 277–88. Cologne: Gitarre und Laute Verlagsgesellschaft, 1980.

Keahey, T. Herman, & Conrad Douglas. *Johannes Prioris: Opera Omnia*. Corpus Mensurabilis Musicae 90. Neuhausen-Stuttgart: American Institute of Musicology/Hänssler Verlag, 1985.

Kiang, Dawson. "Josquin Desprez and a Possible Portrait of the Ottoman Prince Jem in Cappella Sistina Ms.41." *Bibliothèque d'humanisme et Renaissance* 54 (1992), 411–26.

Kraft, Isabel. *Einstimmigkeit um 1500: Der Chansonnier Paris, BnF f. fr. 12744*. Beihefte zum Archiv für Musikwissenschaft 64, with attached CD. Wiesbaden: Franz Steiner, 2009.

Labande-Mailfert, Yvonne. *Charles VIII. Le vouloir et la destinée*. Paris: Fayard, 1986.

Lemonnier, Henri. *La France sous Charles VIII, Louis XII et François Ier (1492–1547). Tome V. Première partie. Les guerres d'Italie*. In *Histoire de France illustrée, depuis les origines jusqu'à la révolution*, edited by Ernest Lavisse. Paris: Hachette, 1900–11, reprinted New York: AMS Press, 1969.

Litterick, Louise. "Prioris, Johannes." In *Grove Music Online* (http://www.oxfordmusiconline.com), accessed on 03/17/2014.

Lockwood, Lewis, editor. *A Ferrarese Chansonnier. Roma, Biblioteca Casanatense 2856, «Canzoniere di Isabella d'Este»*. Lucca: Libreria Musicale Italiana, 2002.

———. "Music at Ferrara in the Period of Ercole I d'Este." *Studi musicali* 1 (1972), 101–31.

———. *Music in Renaissance Ferrara, 1400–1505: The Creation of a Musical Center in the Fifteenth Century*. Oxford: Oxford University Press, 1984.

Lowinsky, Edward E. "Ascanio Sforza's Life: A Key to Josquin's Biography and an Aid to the Chronology of his Works." In *Josquin des Prez: Proceedings of the International Josquin Festival-Conference held at The Juilliard School at Lincoln Center in New York City, 21–25 June 1971*, edited by Edward E. Lowinsky with Bonnie J. Blackburn, 31–75. London: Oxford University Press, 1976.

Luisi, Francesco. "Ben venga maggio. Dalla canzone a ballo alla Commedia di maggio." In *La musica a Firenze al tempo di Lorenzo il Magnifico*, edited by Piero Gargiulo, 195–218. Quaderni della Rivista Italiana di Musicologia 30. Florence: Leo S. Olschki (1993).

Macey Patrick, et al. "Josquin (Lebloitte dit) des Prez [Josse, Gosse, Joskin, Jossequin, Josquinus, Jodocus, Judocus, Juschino; Desprez, des Près, des Prés, de Prés, a Prato, de Prato, Pratensis]." In Grove Music Online (http://www.oxfordmusiconline.com), accessed on 10/13/2014.

Maissen, Thomas. "Ein Mythos wird Realität: Die Bedeutung der französischen Geschichte für das Florenz der Medici." In *Der Medici Papst Leo X. und Frankreich. Politik, Kultur und Familiengeschäfte in der europäischen Renaissance*, edited by Götz-Rüdiger Tewes & Michael Rohlmann, 117–35. Spätmittelalter und Reformation, neue Reihe 19. Tübingen: Mohr Siebeck, 2002.

Maniates, Maria R. "Combinative Chansons in the Dijon Chansonnier." *Journal of the American Musicological Society* 23 (1970), 28–81.

———. "Combinative Chansons in the Escorial Chansonnier." *Musica Disciplina* 29 (1975), 61–125.

———, editor. *The Combinative Chanson: An Anthology*. Recent Researches in the Music of the Renaissance 77. Madison, WI: A-R Editions, Inc., 1989.

Paris, Gaston, and Auguste Gevaert, editors. *Chansons du XVe siècle, publiées d'après le manuscrit de la Bibliothèque nationale de Paris*. Paris: Firmin Didot, 1875.

Picker, Martin, editor. *The Chanson Albums of Marguerite of Austria. MSS 228 and 11239 of the Bibliothèque Royale de Belgique, Brussels*. Berkeley & Los Angeles: University of California Press, 1965.

Piette, Ruth E. "Florence, Biblioteca Nazionale Centrale, Magliabechi XIX, 176: Transcription and Commentary." Master's diss., University of California at Berkeley, 1957.

Powers, Wendy J. "The Music Manuscript Fondo Magliabechi xix.178 of the Biblioteca Nazionale Centrale, Florence: A Study of the Changing Role of the Chanson in Late Fifteenth-Century Florence." Ph.D. diss., Columbia University, 1994.

Rahn, Douglas J. "Melodic and Textual Types in French Monophonic Song, ca. 1500." Ph.D. diss., Columbia University, 1978.

Reynolds, Christopher A. *Papal Patronage and the Music of St. Peter's, 1380–1513*. Berkeley, Los Angeles & London: University of California Press, 1995.

Rifkin, Joshua. "Pietrequin Bonnel and Ms. 2794 of the Biblioteca Riccardiana." *Journal of the American Musicological Society* 29 (1976), 284–96.

———."Referat Brown—Diskussion." In *Formen und Probleme der Überlieferung mehrstimmiger Musik im Zeitalter Josquins Desprez*, edited by Ludwig Finscher, 122. Wolfenbütteler Forschungen 6; Quellenstudien zur Musik der Renaissance 1. Munich: Kraus International Publications, 1981.

———, et al. "Compère, Loyset." In *Grove Music Online* (http://www.oxfordmusiconline.com), accessed on 09/24/2014.

Rigo, Paola. "Donà, Girolamo." In *Dizionario Biografico degli Italiani* 40, 1991, online at: http://www.treccani.it/enciclopedia/girolamo-dona_%28Dizionario-Biografico%29/, accessed on 02/10/2015.

Sherr, Richard. *Papal Music Manuscripts in the Late Fifteenth and Early Sixteenth Centuries*. Renaissance Manuscript Studies 5. Neuhausen: American Institute of Musicology/Hänssler Verlag, 1996.

———. "Pintelli, Johannes." In *Grove Music Online* (http://www.oxfordmusiconline.com), accessed on 07/28/2013.

Stewart, Rebecca. *Josquin des Prez: Missa 'Lesse faire a mi.'* Liner notes to the recording Ricercar 159166 (1996).

Strohm, Reinhard & Emma Kempson. "Isaac [Ysaak, Ysac, Yzac], Henricus [Heinrich; Arrigo d'Ugo; Arrigo Tedesco]." In *Grove Music Online* (http://www.oxfordmusiconline.com), accessed on 02/18/2015.

Wegman, Rob, et al. "Agricola [Ackerman], Alexander." In *Grove Music Online* (http://www.oxfordmusiconline.com), accessed on 02/16/2015.

Wolff, Arthur S. "The Chansonnier Biblioteca Casanatense 2856: Its History, Purpose, and Music." Ph.D. diss., North Texas State University, 1970.

Zazulia, Emily. "'Corps contre corps,' voix contre voix: Conflicting Codes of Discourse in the Combinative Chanson." *Early Music* 38 (2010), 347–59.

Zuckerman Wesner, Amanda. "The Chansons of Loyset Compère: A Model for a Changing Aesthetic." In *Music in Renaissance Cities and Courts: Studies in Honor of Lewis Lockwood*, edited by Jessie A. Owens & Anthony M. Cummings, 483–501. Warren, MI: Harmonie Park Press, 1997.

"BOTH SCHOLLERS AND PRACTICIONERS": THE PEDAGOGY OF ETHICAL SCHOLARSHIP AND MUSIC IN THOMAS MORLEY'S *PLAINE AND EASIE INTRODUCTION TO PRACTICALL MUSICKE**

JOSEPH ARTHUR MANN

I would counsell you diligentlie to peruse those waies which my loving Maister [...] M. *Bird*, and M. *Alphonso* in a vertuous contention in love betwixt themselves made upon the plainsong of *Miserere*, but a contention, as I saide, in love: which caused them strive everie one to surmount another, without malice, envie, or backbiting: but by great labour, studie and paines, e[a]ch making other censure of that which they had done. Which contention of theirs (speciallie without envie) caused them both become excellent in that kind, and winne such a name, and gaine such credite, as wil never perish so long as Musicke indureth. Therefore, there is no waie readier to cause you become perfect, then to contend with some one or other, not in malice (for so is your contention uppon passion, not for love of vertue) but in love, shewing your adversarie your worke, and not skorning to bee corrected of him, and to amende your fault if hee speake with reason [...].[1]

Introduction

Scholarship on the musical aspects of Thomas Morley's *Plaine and Easie Introduction to Practicall Musicke*, published in 1597, has appeared periodically

---

* I owe much thanks to Andrew H. Weaver for all of his helpful criticism, insight, and advice in the process of developing this research and transforming it into a conference paper and then an article. I am also very grateful for the fair criticism and constructive comments from the anonymous reviewers for *Musica Disciplina* and from Stanley Boorman. All of these ethical scholars have helped make this article much better than it was when they first read it.

1. Morley, *Plaine and Easie Introduction*, 115. This is hereafter cited as Morley, *Introduction*. In transcribing the quotations presented in this article, I have standardized the usage of letters, such as "v" and "u," to improve readability, and I have opted not to include the italic formatting used in the original sources when it was used as the default for the passage. Instead, I have formatted the passage in regular font and placed in italics any words that were set off in the original by not being set in italics.

since the beginning of the 20th century,[2] and a new scholarly edition of the treatise will soon appear in print. Research that extends beyond the purely musical aspects of the work, however, is still in its infancy. Currently, the *Plaine and Easie Introduction* has yet to be examined as a work of literature, and any possible extra-musical functions of the work remain a mystery. We know, for example, that the treatise is in dialogue form, and excellent work has been done by Cristle Collins Judd concerning the use of musical examples in relation to dialogue format,[3] but at present no attempt has been made to define the style of the dialogue, or to associate that specific style with Morley's authorial goals. Surprisingly, we do not even have a comprehensive understanding of why Morley published the *Plaine and Easie Introduction*; it certainly was intended as a beginner's guide to performing music, but the assumption that this intention was the only one motivating Morley overlooks his fervent complaints against backbiting and ignorance, which appear prominently in the preface and throughout the work. Indeed, none of the literature on the *Plaine and Easie Introduction* even acknowledges that these consistent complaints exist.

Furthermore, the assumption that this work is just a music tutor—albeit a very well-made one—is also inadequate as an explanation for why Morley chose dialogue form. While this form did have a certain association with musical pedagogy in other countries, Italy specifically, it was never popular in England for discussions of music, and when it does appear in Morley's treatise and in one by Thomas Robinson published in 1603,[4] it does so in a style that was uncommon in musical treatises of other countries. Understanding Morley's reasons for choosing dialogue form for this work, based on the connotations for the form at the time, as well as its meaning for Morley himself, while taking into account his intentions behind the frequent complaints against unethical scholarship, will add a new dimension to our current understanding of why Morley wrote his *Plaine and Easie Introduction*, and a new perspective on the work as a whole.

---

2. Beginning with Sir John Stainer's lecture published in 1902, and ending most recently with the article by David Stern, "Thomas Morley," from 2010. Rebecca Herissone, *Music Theory* is perhaps the most extensive discussion of the theoretical content of the treatise and its legacy.

3. Cristle Collins Judd, "Music in Dialogue." Jessie Ann Owens, "You Can Tell a Book," is an excellent article, on the significance of printed format in the treatise and other theoretical works from England. Roger Harmon, "From Themistocles to Philomathes" also provides a detailed examination of the philosophical roots of the character names in the treatise.

4. Thomas Robinson, *The Schoole of Musicke*.

Therefore, it is the purpose of this article to expand the scholarly literature on Morley's *Plaine and Easie Introduction* beyond the realm of music theory and purely musical studies by examining the context, function, form, and content of the treatise from a literary perspective. The evidence derived from this examination reveals that, in addition to purely musical instruction, ethical/moral pedagogy constitutes a significant component of the *Plaine and Easie Introduction* and explains Morley's consistent complaints against unethical musicians, his choice of dialogue form, and those contents of the treatise that go beyond practical instruction.

More specifically, this article begins by examining the state of the musical community in late 16th- and early 17th-century England, the context in which Morley conceived and wrote his treatise, and then briefly examines Morley's treatise in relation to that context, while a second section uses Morley's own words to establish his motives for publishing the *Plaine and Easie Introduction*. Turning next to the form of the treatise, an examination of Renaissance styles of dialogue demonstrates that the *Plaine and Easie Introduction* is a Platonian dialogue, a style which was and is intimately associated with ethical and moral instruction: examination of 16th-century musical dialogues and dialogues on ethics suggests that Morley most likely chose the Platonian style because of his familiarity with ethical dialogues, rather than for any commercial reasons or because of the influence of contemporary music texts. The last two sections of this article address the content of the dialogue itself and attempt to show that a framework of ethical and moral instruction exists within Morley's *Plaine and Easie Introduction*. Indeed, several elements of the dialogue serve no appreciable function from the standpoint of musical instruction, but are nevertheless integral elements within the framework of ethical/moral instruction.

Morley and Music in the Context of late 16th-Century/Early 17th-Century England

By the end of the 16th century, life as a musician in English society was one of many enemies and few friends. After attempting to regulate professional musical activity, by requiring steady employment in the house of a noble or registration and licensing through government officials, the English government's "Acte for punyshment of rogues, vagabonds and sturdy beggars" of 1597 essentially outlawed freelance musical activities (i.e., minstrelsy) altogether.⁵ Along with the legal attacks on minstrels, works such as Stephan Gosson's *The Schoole of Abuse*⁶ and Philip Stubs' *The Anatomie of Abuses* encouraged readers to see music itself and all those associated with it as impediments to the creation and maintenance of a virtuous society. According to Stubs,

> Al good minstrels, sober, & chast musicions, (speaking of such drunken sockets, & baudy *Parasites* as raunge the Countries, roming & singing of unclean, corupt and filthy songs in taverns, Alehouses, Innes, & other publike assemblies) may dance the wilde Moris through a needles eye. For how should they beare chast minds seeing that their excercise is the pathway to all Baudry & filthines [...] who bee baudier knaves then they'[?]: Who uncleaner then they'[?]: Who more licentious, and looser minded then they'[?]: Who more incontinent then they'[?]: And brieflie, who more inclined to all kinde of insolency and lewdnes then they'[?]:⁷

In response to these fundamental attacks on their profession and their moral quality, scholars such as Thomas Lodge, with his *Protogenes Can Know Apelles* (1579), and John Case, with his *The Praise of Musicke* (1586), came to the defense of musicians and music and established a sort of equilibrium between defenders and detractors. Indeed, William Byrd was grateful enough for Case's defense that he wrote and published a six-voice madrigal setting of *A Gratification unto Master John Case, for his Learned Book, Lately made in the Praise of Musicke* (1586? See note 8, below), a text by Thomas Watson that casts the opponent of music as "the senceles [senseless] foole, & Barbarous Scithyan, of our dayes" and suggests that in Case's work "Here may the solemne Stoycks finde, And that Rude Marsia [Marsyas] wanteth skil, wanteth skill, against Apollos sweete concent, the Nurse of good, the scourge of ill," and declares "Let Envy barke against the starres, let Folly sayle which way she please," because Case's "quill hath stoode fayre Musickes frend."⁸

---

5. Christopher Marsh, *Music and Society*, 73–75.
6. Stephan Gosson, *The Schoole of Abuse*, (1579, and reprinted in 1587).
7. Philip Stubs, *The Anatomie of Abuses* (1583, reprinted in 1584, 1585, and 1595), 128.
8. William Byrd, *A Gratification unto Master John Case, for his Learned Book, Lately made in the Praise of Musicke*. Only one part from the work survives. In addition to being well-known for his collections of poetry, Thomas Watson also published *The First Sett, of Italian Madrigalls Englished,* which contains Italian madrigals that have had their Italian texts replaced with English paraphrases by Watson and two additional madrigals by Byrd. The publication date on this work remains uncertain. *Early English Books Online* dates the work to 1586 because it mentions the *Praise of Musicke* as a recent work, and also attributes the book to Case. New Grove, however, in "Case, John," dates it to 1589, presumably because the *Apologia musices* by Case was published in 1588—and the authorship of the *Praise of Musicke* is still debated.

Other practicing musicians felt they could add little to the debate: one such was George Kirbye, who commented that

> It were a thing very unnecessary [...] for mee [...] to speake any thing in commendation & praise of musicke, considering (besides that many learned men have learnedly written in commendation thereof) the examples of times past, and our owne experience every day, doth give sufficient testimonie both of the pleasure and proffit that it bringeth to a distressed & melancholy mind. Also I think it convenient not to answere (otherwise then with silence) to those (more sencelesse then brute beastes) that with open mouthes doe in-weigh, & speake all the evill they can against that excellent knowledge.[9]

That they did not need to contribute to the debate, however, did not prevent practical musicians from feeling frustration over the state of their profession, and gratitude for not having been affected by it to a greater extent. Thomas Weelkes, in the dedication of his *Balletts and Madrigals* (1598), for example, was particularly thankful to his patron in light of the "infamy" and "povertie" that had recently befallen his fellow musicians:

> Right worshipfull, it is no small comfort the Musicke professors conceive, when they consider the ever misdeeming multitude to brand them with infamy, whom the most Honorable spirits have alwaies honored: and although povertie hath debarred them their fellow arts mens companie, yet nature hath set their better part at libertie, to delight them that love Musicke. Amongst so many worthy men dayly labouring to call home againe the banished Philomele, whose purest blood the impure Minstralsie hath stained, I must presume to remember [that you support musicians].[10]

Within Weelkes' gratitude also lies the careful distancing of learned musicians from the "impure Minstralsie" who "hath stained" the pure blood of the "musicke professors;" the battle-lines over music in late 16th-century England were not as simply drawn as public and government versus music and musicians, but included a significant upper-class and lower-class factional division amongst musicians, as well as a division between those who were lucky enough to have secure positions and those who were not (which tended also to be a generational divide).

---

9. George Kirbye, *The First Set of English Madrigals*, [p. iii].
10. Thomas Weelkes, *Balletts and Madrigals*, [p. iii].

Indeed, evidence suggests that musicians who were publishing works and employed by patrons were certainly aware of the state of musical life in the country, but felt the impact most intimately in the form of backbiting from musicians who could not find the positions they desired and who desperately sought recognition from a divided society that was both saturated with quality musicians and weary of the perceived immoral influences that the wrong kinds of music or the wrong kinds of musicians could exert on them. Robert Jones, for example, describes the precarious position of contemporary musicians, in the dedication of his *Second Booke of Songs and Ayres* (1601), but then goes on to blame the selfishness and jealousy of detractors as the reason for their lack of success:

> Our statures are not set above danger; wee lie lowe, fit for everie foote to treade upon: our place is the ground, there is nothing beneath us, and yet detraction will pull us lower, if wee have not good aspects. They will find meanes to digge and let us downe into the earth, and burie us before our time: This is the cause of patronage, and this is the persecution of them that would ingrosse all Glorie into their owne hands. But see the rage of these men, they bite the fruites themselves should feede upon. Vertue would bring forth manie *Children* [pieces of music] but they hold them in the wombe that they dare not come out. As the covetous man besiegeth all the land about him, with statutes, fines, and bands, and other such civill warre: so doth the ambitious intrap the little portion of anie commendations that maie fall besides him. And like the mercilesse Souldiers; the Castles they cannot take, they blow up. They are as sparing of everie small remenant of credit, as if it were laide up in common-banke; and the more were given awaie, the lesse would come to their shares. They are miserable men, I will only brand them with this marke, and let them goe. they were Eagles, if they did not catch flyes, as they are; they are great things, much lesse then nothing. For my part, I will not contend with them, I desire no applause or commendations: let them have the fame of Ecchoes and sounds, and let me be a Bird in your Cage, to sing to my selfe and you.[11]

According to Jones, the "miserable men" who detract from other musicians prevent those musicians from bringing forth great works because, like "mercilesse Souldiers," they seek to destroy what they could not or would not have. Three years earlier, John Farmer addressed the infighting of the English musical community by calling for unity towards the common goal of improving the honor of the country:

---

11. Robert Jones, *The Second Booke of Songs and Ayres*, [p. iii].

> To conclude, I so much love perfect harmony, as I earnestly entreate all the professed in Musicke to fly discord amongst themselves: though in composing of songes, it may be well taken, beseeching them so farre to fly selfe-opinion also, that ayming all of them at their Countries honor, not their owne glory, they may by this meanes and in this manner outstrip any stranger, and make England as famous in Musitions, as it is and hath beene for soldiers.[12]

John Dowland also noticed the infighting in England, in spite of having lived outside the country from 1594 until approximately 1609, and in the "Epistle to the Reader" of his *Third and Last Booke of Songs* (1603) he argues not for the inclusive unity for which Farmer hopes, but an exclusive unity that would oust the backbiters from their community:

> As in a hive of bees al labour alike to lay up honey opposing them selves against none but fruitles drones; so in the house of learning and fame, all good indevourers should strive to ad somewhat that is good, not malicing one an other, but altogether bandying against the idle and malicious ignorant.[13]

Nearly a decade after their first complains against backbiters, both Jones and Dowland again expressed their frustration with the musical community. This time, however, they both not only mark their opponents as arrogant, unfair critics, but they also point out their practical musical deficiencies. In the preface to *A Pilgrimes Solace*, for example, Dowland claims that

> So have I againe found strange entertainment since my returne [to England]; especially by the opposition of two sorts of people that shroude themselves under the title of musicians. The first are some simple Cantors, or vocall singers, who though they seeme excellent in their blinde Division-making, are meerely ignorant, even in the first elements of musicke, and also in the true order of the mutation of the *Hexachord* in the *systeme*, (which hath ben approved by all the learned and skilfull men of Christendome, this 800 yeeres,) yet doe these fellowes give their verdict of me behinde my backe, and say, what I doe is after the old manner: but I will speake openly to them, and would have them know that the proudest Cantor of them, dares not oppose himselfe face to face against me. The second are young men, professors of the Lute, who vaunt themselves to the disparagement of such as have beene before their time,

---

12. John Farmer, *The First Set of English Madrigals*, [p. iv].
13. John Dowland, *The Third and Last Booke of Songs*, [p. iv].

(wherein I my selfe am a party) that there never was the like of them. To these men I say little, because of my love and hope to see some deedes ensue their brave wordes.[14]

Similarly, Jones declares in the lengthy preface "To All Musicall Murmurers" from his *A Musicall Dreame* that

> Thou, whose eare itches with the varietie of opinion, hearing thine owne sound, as the Ecchoe reverberating others substance, and unprofitable in it selfe, shewes to the World comfortable noyse, though to thy owne use little pleasure, by reason of uncharitable censure. I speake to thee musicall *Momus*, thou from whose nicetie, numbers as easily passe, as drops fall in the showre, but with less profite. I compare thee to the hie way dust that flies into mens eyes, and will not thence without much trouble, for thou in thy dispersed judgment, not onely art offensive to seeing knowledge, but most faulty false to deserving industry, picking moates out of the most pure Blisse, and smoothing the plainest velvet, when onely thine owne opinion is more wrinckled and more vitious in itselfe, then grosser soyle, so that as a brush infected with filth, thou rather soylest then makest perfect anyway. I have stood at thine elbow, and heard thee prophane even Musickes best Note, and with they untunde relish Sol Fade most ignobly [...] but understand me thou unskilfull descanter, derive from that Note of Plaine Song charitable numbers, and thou shalt find harsh voices are often a Note above Ela reduced by truer judgment, which I bereave thee of, knowing thy Rules, are as our new come Lutes, being of many stringes, not easily used, useless in adventure, till practise put forward into deserving Division [...] It is hard if al this paines reape not good commendations, and it is water wrung out of a Flint in thee, sith thou never thinkst well of any, and wert in thy selfe so unskilfull ever, as thy Tutor from the first howre could never make thee sing in Tune; be as thou art a lumpe of deformity without fashion, bredde in the bowels of disdaine, and brought forth by bewitcht *Megaera*, the fatall Widwife [midwife] to all true merite. Give me leave to depart, or if not, without it I am gone, carelesse of thy censuring, and fully perswaded thou canst not thinke well, and therefore art curst in thy Cradle, never to be but cruell, and being borne with teeth in thy head, bitst every one harmeles in this or what else honest industry, makes thy eare gossip too.[15]

Like all the Momists mentioned in previous instances, Dowland's and Jones' detractors are eager to build their careers on the ashes of their predecessors,

---

14. John Dowland, *A Pilgrimes Solace*, [p. iv].
15. Robert Jones, *A Musicall Dreame*, [p. iv].

but here we see that they were also considered (whether fairly or not) to be as deficient musically as they were morally, an idea which also appears, as we shall see, in Morley's treatise.

Turning finally to Morley himself, we find him as aware of the tensions in his community and as willing to address them as any of his contemporaries. Just as Byrd declares Case's defeat of the anti-music stoics, for example, Morley's master Gnorimus character is surprised to hear that the student character Philomathes wants to learn about music, because "I have heard you so much speake against that art, as to terme it a corrupter of good manners, & an allurement to vices, for which many of your companions termed you a stoick."[16] Morley's use of the term "stoick" here could be a direct reference to the *Schoole of Abuse*, where Gosson claims that "I make juste reckoning to bee held for a *Stoike*, in dealing so hardly with these people."[17] In any case, by making his student character admit the error of his ways as an anti-music supporter, saying that "I am so farre changed, as of a *Stoick* I would willingly make a *Pythagorian*,"[18] Morley wins a fictional victory of his own over the anti-music movement, while at the same time (as will be discussed in greater detail below) preparing his student to be reborn as an ethical and technically proficient musician.

A much larger frustration for Morley, however, comes from the assaults and arrogance of ignorant musicians who enjoy finding fault in others, but will not recognize it in themselves. Just as Robert Jones spoke out against those musicians who "would ingrosse all Glorie into their owne Hands"[19] and "never think it well of any,"[20] Morley complains repeatedly about the many who

> will read it [the *Plaine and Easie Introduction*], not so much for anie pleasure or profit they looke for in it, as to finde some thing whereat to repine, or take occasion of backbyting [...] upon mallice, or for ostentation of his owne knowledge, or for ignorance [...] do either in huggermugger or openly calumniate that which either he understandeth not, or then maliciously wresteth to his own sense.[21]

---

16. Morley, *Introduction*, 2.
17. Gosson, *The Schoole of Abuse*, 52.
18. Morley, *Introduction*, 2.
19. Jones, *Second Booke*, [p. iii].
20. Jones, *Dreame*, [p. iv].
21. Morley, *Introduction*, [p. vi].

Morley is also willing, as Jones and Dowland were, to point out the musical insufficiencies of those who would criticize his methods. According to Morley, some backbiters had already claimed that he was wasting his time by thoroughly discussing theoretical issues that are no longer of any practical use. In response, Morley argues that it is necessary to understand the theory of the past if works from the past are to be appreciated and studied:

> Some have beene so foolish as to say that I have emploied much travell in vaine in seeking out the depth of those moodes and other things which I have explained, and have not stucke to say that they be in no use, and that I can write no more then they know already. Surely what they know already I know not, but if they account the moodes, ligatures, pricks of devision and alteration, augmentation, diminution and proportions, things of no use, they may as well account the whole arte of musicke of no use, seeing that in the knowledge of them consisteth the whole or greatest part of the knowledge of pricksong. And although it be true that the proportions have not such use in musicke in that forme as they be nowe used, but that the practise may be perfect without them, yet seeing they have beene in common use with the musicians of former time, it is necessarie for us to know them, if we meane to make any profit of their works. But those men who think they know enough already, when (God knoweth) they can scarce sing their part with the wordes, be like unto those who having once superficiallie red the Tenors of *Littleton* or *Justinians institutes,* thinke that they have perfectlie learned the whole law, and then being injoyned to discusse a case, do at length perceive their own ignorance and beare the shame of their falsely conceaved opinions.[22]

Therefore, Morley's detractors were just as ignorant and technically deficient as Dowland's ignorant cantors, and both groups would quickly find themselves wanting when faced with practical challenges to their knowledge.

Interestingly, no evidence of backbiting against Morley and his contemporaries is currently extant, except in their own accounts of it and responses to it as given above. This lack of surviving sources from backbiters makes sense, however, considering that the criticism was most likely coming from a group of musicians who were not able to find patrons or publish works, as a result of the depressed nature of the musical community at the time.

---

22. Morley, *Introduction,* 183. Thomas Littleton wrote one of the first printed texts on English law, his *Tenures* (1482).

Therefore, it is likely that the backbiting was verbal and that Morley and his contemporaries were made aware of it through hearsay; indeed, the word backbiting itself implies talking about someone behind their back, and Dowland even says "yet doe these fellowes give their verdict of me behinde my backe."[23] Finally, the restrictions on music publishing, and publishing in general, in Elizabethan England would also decrease the likelihood that slanderous works would be published at all, even if the backbiters could afford such an effort.

In His Own Words: Morley's Reasons for Publishing the *Plaine and Easie Introduction*

Being unable to address their attackers directly, Morley and his contemporaries appealed to the virtuous members of their community and to their patrons for defense and for support against the ignorant rabble. Morley himself took the campaign one step further and not only spoke out against the infighting of the time, but attempted to reform it through musical and ethical instruction. With the musical context of late 16th-century England in mind, and having had a preview of Morley's criticism of unethical, ignorant musicians, we turn now to Morley's own stated reasons for writing the *Plaine and Easie Introduction*. To find them, we turn to the introduction and conclusion of the treatise, which represent the only extant account from Morley regarding his reasons for writing it, the contemporary reaction, and his rationale for its structure.

According to Morley, his principal reason for writing the treatise was

> First, the earnest intreatie of my friends daily requesting, importuning, and as it were adjuring me by the love of my contrie, which next unto the glorie of God, ought to be most deere to every man. Which reason so often tolde, and repeted to mee by them, chiefly caused mee yield to their honest request in taking in hand this worke which now I publish to the viewe of the worlde [...] Lastly, the solitarie life which I lead (being compelled to keepe at home) caused mee be glad to finde anything wherein to keepe my selfe exercised for the benefite of my contrie.[24]

---

23. Dowland, *Solace*, [p. iv].
24. Morley, *Introduction*, [p. v].

Here Morley repeatedly emphasizes his desire to contribute to the benefit of his country as the primary goal for his agreeing to undertake writing the *Plaine and Easie Introduction*. Morley's secondary goal in writing the treatise was

> Not so much seeking thereby any name or glorie, (though no honest minde do contemne that also, and I might more largely by other meanes and lesse labour have obtained) as in some sort to further the studies of them, who (being indewed with good naturall wittes, and well inclined to learne that divine Art of Musick) are destitute of sufficient masters.[25]

The work is not simply for students who wish to learn, but specifically for students who already have masters who are insufficient. Indeed, Morley emphasizes the quality of their masters as more significant than their own inclination towards music when he states the latter parenthetically and the former within the main body of the sentence, just as he also emphasizes the sufficiency of available masters rather than the lack of any masters at all.

Morley also believes that his treatise will help these insufficient masters become proficient, contributing members of the community, and he hopes that their reformation will be one of the benefits of the treatise, going so far as to say that it was the effect that he meant and the benefit for which he had hoped:

> if any at all owe mee any thanks for the great paines which I have taken, they be in my iudgement, those who taught that which they knew not, and may here if they will learne. But if the effect do not answere to my good meaning, and if manie do not reape that benefit which I hoped; yet there wil be no reason why I should be blamed, who have done what I could, and given an occasion to others of better judgement and deeper skill then my selfe to doe the like.[26]

In fact, he asserts that insufficient masters are the ones who should benefit the most from the treatise, and he also hopes that the *Plaine and Easie Introduction* will inspire other better musicians to write works for the improvement of the community.

At the same time that his treatise will improve the abilities of those who are willing to learn, Morley makes it clear that he has no desire even to acknowledge those individuals who criticize unjustly, argue ignorantly, and/or

---

25. Ibid.
26. Ibid., [p. vi].

have inflated opinions of themselves. Not only does he repeatedly cast them as his sworn enemies and focus overwhelmingly on pointing out their flaws, but by refusing to acknowledge them, just as Jones did in the preface to his *A Musicall Dreame*, Morley effectively expels them from his musical community (an action which, as we shall see, he intends his readers to emulate):

> I doubt not but diverse also will read it, not so much for anie pleasure or profit they looke for in it, as to finde some thing whereat to repine, or take occasion of backbyting. Such men I warne […]
>
> But if any man, either upon mallice, or for ostentation of his owne knowledge, or for ignorance […] do either in huggermugger or openly calumniate that which either he understandeth not, or then maliciously wresteth to his own sense, he […] shall finde that I have a tongue also: […] There have also been some, who (knowing their own insufficiencie, and not daring to disallow, nor being able to improve any thing in the booke) have neverthelesse gone about to discredite both mee and it another waie, affirming that I have by setting out thereof maliciously gone about to take away the livings from a number of honest poore men, who live (and that honestly) upon teaching not halfe of that which in this booke may be found. But to answere those malicious caterpillers, [(] who live upon the paines of other men,) this booke will be so farre from the hinderance of anie, that by the contrarie, it will cause those whome they alledge to be thereby damnified, to be more able to give reason for that which they do: Whereas before they either did it at haphazard, or for all reasons alledged, that they were so taught […] And as for those ignorant Asses, who take upon them to lead others, none being more blinde then themselves, and yet without any reason, before they have seene their workes, wil condemne other men, I overpasse them, as being unworthie to be nominated, or that any man should vouchsafe to aunswere them: for they be in deede such as doing wickedly hate the light for feare they should be espyed.[27]

And again, as mentioned above, Morley associates the superficial musical knowledge of his critics with a resistance to and hostility towards his attempt to enhance their knowledge:

> But those men who think they know enough already, when (God knoweth) they can scarce sing their part with the wordes, be like unto those who having once superficiallie red the Tenors of *Littleton* or *Justinians institutes*, thinke that they have perfectlie learned the whole law,

---

27. Ibid.

and then being injoyned to discusse a case, do at length perceive their own ignorance and beare the shame of their falsely conceaved opinions But to such kind of men I do not wright, for as a man having brought a horse to the water cannot compel him to drink except he list [i.e. unless he wants to], so may I write a booke to such a man but cannot compell him to reade it: But this difference is betwixt the horse and the man, that the horse though hee drinke not will notwithstanding returne quietly with his keeper to the stable, and not kicke at him for bringing him fourth: our man by the contrarie will not onelie not reade that which might instruct him, but also wil backbite and maligne him, who hath for his and other mens benefit undertaken great labor and endured much paine, more then for any privat gaine or commoditie in particular redounding [rebounding] to himself.[28]

As a testament to the intensity of Morley's aversion to these "malicious caterpillers" and "ignorant Asses," every page of the introductory material of the treatise—the dedication, the poetic endorsements, and the preface—contains references to and statements against these unethical scholars. Incredibly, almost half of the "To the courteous Reader" section is focused on this subject, with more space dedicated to unethical scholarship than the discussion of authorial methods, motives, and content combined![29] Not only does Morley make his aversion to these ignorant scholars clear, but he also incites his readers to assume a similar stance when he states that "I overpasse them, as being unworthie to be nominated, or that any man should vouchsafe to aunswere them."

The Dialogue in 16th-century Europe: Platonian versus Ciceronian

Knowing that Morley was displeased with the low moral quality of the musical community in which he worked, and that service to his country and a reformation of insufficient masters were stated goals of the treatise, we may now turn to an examination of Renaissance dialogical styles and how Morley's expressed goals influenced his choice of the form and style of the *Plaine and Easie Introduction* in relation to the Renaissance conception of the dialogue as a literary form.

Essentially, there were two main dialogical styles in which treatises were set during the Renaissance: the Platonian and the Ciceronian. The Platonian

---

28. Ibid., 183.
29. Ibid., [pp. iii–vi].

literary dialogue (modeled after the dialogues of Plato) was designed to teach knowledge and the ethical use of knowledge to novice readers through the interactions of a group of fictional interlocutors (often with Greek names) that always consists of a master/teacher character and one or more student characters who participate in the dialogue in lieu of the reader. As the dialogue progresses the student character or characters develop morally and intellectually, and it was believed that, through observing this transformation, the reader would likewise develop into an ethical, intellectually competent scholar. Platonian dialogues also tend to forego long descriptions of dramatic setting or location because the primary concern of the style is the facilitation of scholarly growth rather than the creation of dramatic interest.[30]

Conversely, the Ciceronian style emphasizes the dramatic elements of the dialogue through the use of real-life historical figures as characters and detailed explanations of the location and dramatic setting of the dialogue. Unlike in the Platonian dialogue, characters are presented as approximate intellectual equals, and there is little or no consideration for the ethical application of the information exposed through the dialogue; rather, the emphasis is on civic discourse, rhetorical skill, and finding the most logical argument. The intellectual maturity of Ciceronian characters also shifts the focus of the dialogue from the development of the characters (as with the Platonian style) to the expression and debate of ideas, so that in this style the reader does not learn with the characters but from them through observation.[31]

Therefore, given his didactic intention, Morley, in constructing his treatise, adhered to the parameters of the Platonian style exactly, including the use of fictional characters with Greek names for his interlocutors, the lack of emphasis on the location and dramatic action, and the experienced-master/novice-student relationship of his characters. The function of the *Plaine and Easie Introduction* also follows the Platonian emphasis on the intellectual and ethical instruction of the ignorant, with Morley's goal being to reform ignorant masters, and "to further the studies of them, who [...] are destitute of sufficient masters,"[32] with "the methode of the booke, [...] I thought most convenient for the capacitie of the learner. [...] I have omitted

---

30. Wilson, *Incomplete Fictions*, 1–34. Buranello, "From the *Locus Amoenus* to the *Locus Ambiguus*," 1–33. Both sources agree regarding the information presented in this and following paragraphs.

31. Wilson, *Incomplete Fictions*, 36–50.

32. Morley, *Introduction*, [p. v].

[…] things onely serving to content the learned, and not for the instruction of the ignorant."[33] Therefore, because the Ciceronian style catered to a sophisticated, intellectually mature audience it would have been unsuitable for Morley's goal of educating beginners and the ignorant.

Moreover, the lack of extant Platonian dialogues on music[34] and the lack of English dialogues on music prior to the publication of the *Plaine and Easie Introduction* increases the probability that Morley's principal reason for choosing the Platonian style was its association with ethical pedagogy, rather than an attempt to directly emulate previous musical authorities. Indeed, England had no tradition of writing musical treatises in dialogue form before Morley's treatise, and in Italy, where dialogues on music were the most common, authors chose the Ciceronian style overwhelmingly.[35] Therefore, the twenty-two extant works written on music in England before 1597 gave Morley no precedent for the use of dialogue form, and only one later English author, Robinson in his *The Schoole of Musicke* (1603), found Morley's use of dialogue form convincing enough to replicate, in spite of the otherwise rampant pirating of the theoretical content of the *Plaine and Easie Introduction* that occurred throughout the 17th century, combined with the proliferation of works targeted at beginners.[36] Furthermore, Zarlino is the only author of a dialogue on music that Morley cites is his list of consulted and cited authorities, and that treatise happens also to be Ciceronian.[37] Therefore, if Morley was being honest and comprehensive in his list of authors consulted, we can only be sure that he may have known of one previous dialogue on music and that it was Ciceronian.

If Morley had no musical models that could have inspired him to write a dialogue in the Platonian style and on which he could have modeled the

---

33. Ibid., [pp. v–vi].

34. Although Vincenso Galilei's *Fronimo* (1584) is technically a Platonian dialogue, there is no evidence currently available to suggest that Morley had ever read it or knew of its existence.

35. See Judd, "Music in Dialogue," 43 for a complete list.

36. Such as Bevin and Campion, who borrowed liberally from the content of Morley's work. Bevin's treatise, *A Briefe and Short Instruction of the Art of Musicke*, attempted to appeal to the same audience of beginners to whom, in part, Morley directed his treatise.

37. Morley does cite several earlier German authors on the last page of his treatise. Among them are Lucas Lossius, who wrote the *Erotemata musicae practicae*, and Sethus Calvisius, author of the *Compendium musicae practicae*. Both of these treatises were written in a question-and-answer format, but do not include any actual dialogue.

Plaine and Easie Introduction, then the question remains of how he became acquainted with the style and with dialogue form in general. The most evident answer is that he was well acquainted with the Platonian style in its original, ethical context, via the dialogues of Plato and through 16th-century imitations of that style by notable authors of works of ethical pedagogy in and outside of England. Throughout the *Plaine and Easie Introduction*, Morley proves himself capable of reading Latin and Greek and in command of a wide array of classical sources. He cites several of Plato's dialogues (including the *Laws*,[38] *Theages*,[39] *Symposium*[40] and *Cratylus*[41]) throughout the treatise and even directly associates music with ethical instruction via a citation of Plato's Republic (referred to as the "common wealth"):

> to begin with *Plato*, he in the seventh booke of his common wealth doth so admire musicke as that he calleth it δαιμόνιον πϱᾶγμα a heavenly thing, καί χϱηςιμου πηος τευ τῶ καλῶ τε και αγαθω ζητησιν and profitable for the seeking out of that which is good and honest.[42]

Furthermore, Roger Harmon has noted several similarities between the beginning of the *Plaine and Easie Introduction* and the openings of a number of Plato's dialogues. He sees the line "Staye (brother *Philomathes*) what haste? Whither go you so fast?"[43] as relating to the openings of the *Republic*, the *Symposium*, the *Lysis*, and the *Phaedrus*. He also sees a connection between the line "But before you goe, I praie you repeat some of the discourses which you had yester night at master *Sophobulus* his banket"[44] and the opening of the *Symposium*.[45]

In addition to a thorough understanding of the dialogues of Plato, however, the names of Morley's characters also hint at specific 16th-century dialogues in the Platonian style. Philomathes, for example, is the student character in James I's Platonian dialogue, *Daemonologie*, which was published the same year as the *Plaine and Easie Introduction* and also happens to be divided

---

38. Morley, *Introduction*, 183.
39. Morley, *Introduction*, Annotation 1, referring to page 2 of the main text.
40. Ibid.
41. Morley, *Introduction*, 118.
42. Ibid., 183.
43. Ibid., 1.
44. Ibid.
45. Harmon, "From Themistocles to Philomathes," 376, n126.

into three books, just as Morley's treatise is divided into three lessons.[46] Not knowing which work was published first in 1597, however, it is also possible that Morley instead took the name from Plato, who uses it in book IX of the *Republic* to describe one who wishes to learn and loves knowledge.[47]

Similarly, Polyphemus is both a character in Homer's *Odyssey* and a character in one of Erasmus' Platonian dialogues, *Cyclops, or the Gospel Bearer* (1529), which was published in England in 1550. Not only does the character appear in Erasmus' dialogue, but the personality of Morley's Polyphemus is very similar to that of Erasmus' Polyphemus. In both works, Polyphemus is arrogant, brutish, easy to quarrel, and otherwise unethical. See page 87 below for Morley's description of Polyphemus; an example of Erasmus' Polyphemus appears below:

> Canni[us:] The gospell is suche a lyke thynge of all this worlde, for after that it hathe ones persed a entered in the veynes of the mynd it altereth, transposeth, and cleane changeth upsodowne the whole state of man, and changeth hym cleane as it were into a nother man.
>
> Polip[hemus:] Ah ha, nowe I wot whereabout ye be, belyke ye thike that I lyve not accordynge to the gospell or as a good gospeller shulde do.
>
> Canni[us:] There is no man can dyssolve this question better than thy self.
>
> Poli[phemus:] Call ye it dissolvynge? Naye and yf a thy age come to dyssolvynge gyve me a good sharpe [battle ax] axe in my hande and I trow I shall dyssolve it well inoughe.
>
> Canni[us:] what would thou do, I praye the, and yf a man shulde say to thy teth [teeth] thou lyest falsely, or elles call the by thy right name knave in englysse.
>
> Poli[phemus:] What wolde I do quod he, that is a question in dede, mary he shulde feele the wayghte of a payre of churlyshe fystes I warrant the.

---

46. James VI and I, *Daemonologie in Forme of a Dialogue*. Significantly, this books is a proof that witchcraft exists, with a discussion of how it may be identified and why it is unethical.

47. C. Strang, "Tripartite souls, Ancient and Modern," 6. It is also possible chronologically, though much less likely, that he could have taken it from the German theorist Venceslaus Philomathes, who wrote a music treatise, *Musicorum libri quatuor*, published in Vienna in 1512 and in Leipzig in 1518 (also 1523, 1534, and 1543): see Robin A. Leaver, *Luther's Liturgical Music*, 39. There is no evidence, however, that Morley knew that the treatise or author existed. (There is, however, a copy of the 1534 edition in London, but there is no evidence to suggest that it was available in England at that time).

Canni[us:] And what and yf a man gave you a good cuffe upon the eare that shulde waye a pounde?

Poliphe[mus:] It were a well geven blowe that wolde advauntage hym [...] I cut not of his head harde by his schuders [i.e., he will not cut his head off, but instead break it].

Canni[us:] yea but good felowe thy gospell boke teacheth the to geve gentle answers, and fayre wordes agayne for fowle, and to hym that geveth the a blowe upon the ryght cheke to holde forth the lyfte.

Poliphe[mus:] I do remember I have red suche a thinge in my boke, but ye must pardone me for I had quyte forgotten it.

Can[nius:] [...] I suppose ye praye very ofte.

Poli[phemus:] That is evyn as very a touche of a pharesey as any can be.

Cannius[:] [...] But thy gospel boke teacheth the to praye contynually, but so that thy prayer come from the bothum of the hart.

Poli[phemus:] [...] I praye sumtyme.

Can[nius:] When [...]?

Poli[phemus:] When it cometh into my mynde, ones or twyse may chaunce in a weke [...].

Canni[us:] Do you kepe the commaundmentes of god?

Polip[hemus:] Nowe ye appose me. Kepe the cmmaundements the, that is a payne in dede [...] there was a certayne gray frere of the order of saynt Franunces [...] whiche never ceased to bable and rayle agaynste the newe testament of Erasmus, I chaunsed to talke with the gentylman pryvatly where no man was present but he and I, and after I had communed a whyle with hym I caught my frere by the polled pate with my left hande and with my right hande I drew out my daggar and I pomelled the knave frere welfauatdly aboute his skonce that I made his face as swollen and as puffed as a puddinge [...]. Now say you is not this a good and a sufficient prove that I faver the gospell. I gave hym absolucion afore he departed out of my handes with this newe testament thyse layde upon his pate as harde as I myght[...].[48]

---

48. Desiderius Erasmus, *Two dyaloges*, 11–18.

The chief difference between these two versions of Polyphemus is that Morley's Polyphemus never improves, while Erasmus' Polyphemus serves as the student character and therefore must show some moral growth by the end of the dialogue. It is also worth mentioning that Morley knew at least some of the works of Erasmus, as he cites him in the second Annotation at the end of the *Plaine and Easie Introduction:* "let him also peruse the notes of *Erasmus* uppon that place, where he taketh up *Gaza* roundlie for his Greeke translation of it."[49]

Furthermore, several of the characters mentioned in passing at the beginning of the *Plaine and Easie Introduction* appear in 16th-century English Platonian dialogues. Eudoxus, who is one of the guests at Sophobulus' banquet (the very banquet that inspires Philomathes to seek out master Gnorimus), appeared as one of two student characters in *The Praise of Solitarinesse* (1577), a Platonian dialogue by Roger Baynes, which discusses "First, what vertue is, and whether a wise man that desireth to live vertuously, ought rather to make choise of Solitariness or Societie."[50]

Likewise, Sophobulus himself appeared as the master character in the Platonian dialogue "Princeps Puer" that appeared in the popular collection *Linguae Latinae Exercitatio* (1539) by Juan Luis Vives. While Vives' dialogues are meant first and foremost to teach Latin, there is also a strong ethical component (as one would expect from a Platonian dialogue). In "Princeps Puer," for example, a bad teacher, Morobulus, tries to convince the student character, Philippus, to abandon his studies and "ride about, chat with the daughters of your august mother, dance, learn the art of bearing arms, play cards or ball, leap and run," which leads Philippus to ask "What! is the study of letters no good?"[51] Sophobulus quickly intervenes, however, to set Philippus on the proper path to virtue, and chastises him when he believes Morobulus' arguments to be logical, but Sophobulus' to be confusing:

> Oh, how happy men would be, if they had the sense and intelligence for good and satisfactory things which they have for frivolous and bad things! Now indeed, on the contrary, at your time of life, it happens that you understand with ease what is trifling, what is inept, nay, even what is insane, such things as those to which Morobulus has exhorted you, and then you regard what I would say on virtue, dignity, and every kind of

---

49. Morley, *Introduction*, Annotation 2.
50. Roger Baynes, *The Prayse of Solitarinesse*, 1.
51. Juan Luis Vives, "Princeps Puer," 173.

praiseworthy thing, as if I were speaking Arabic or Gothic […] You should at least suspend your judgment. Neither acquiesce in the opinions of Morobulus, nor in mine, until you are able to judge as to both.[52]

Finally, it might be argued that, because these names have clear allegorical associations when translated from the Greek (with, for example, Philomathes being the Greek equivalent of naming an English character Love-learning), Morley simply invented them himself and had no knowledge of the Platonian dialogues in which they appear. The abundant proof that Morley was well-read, the frequency with which his characters' names correspond to those that appear in previous works (four of the eight fictional names that appear in the *Plaine and Easie Introduction*), and the fact that besides Morley's treatise none of the 55 extant dialogues from 1597 or earlier borrow Greek names from other dialogues (unless written by the same author) makes it unlikely that he was using these names without being aware at least to some degree of the works in which they originally appeared.

Therefore, a conscious desire to present practical and ethical knowledge to beginners is the best explanation of why Morley would avoid the Ciceronian style of contemporary music treatises (even if he only knew of one), instead allying his treatise with works that focus on or include ethical instruction: Morley's goal was not to seek glory (or money as many authors in the coming century would), but to genuinely improve the quality of musical practice and ethics in his country, "which next unto the glorie of God, ought to be most deere to every man."[53]

Morley's Method of Ethical Pedagogy: Real and Fictional Models of Scholarly Virtue

With Morley's frustrations and the implications of the Platonian dialogue in mind, the content of the treatise takes on a new ethical and moral significance. Ethical instruction relies, at its heart, on examples of positive and negative action, coupled with an explanation of why those actions are categorized as such. Accordingly, throughout the treatise, Morley provides examples of positive and negative actions in the form of real examples drawn from his personal experience and fictional examples that are created through the plot of the dialogue.

---

52. Ibid., 174–75.
53. Morley, *Introduction*, [p. v].

Real Virtue

Morley's real examples of positive scholarly action take the form of references to praiseworthy composers from Morley's own time or drawn from his studies. The most notable of these examples is presented briefly in the second lesson in the form of a story regarding the means by which both William Byrd and Alphonso Ferrabosco (two of Morley's most beloved masters) reached the pinnacle of musical/scholarly perfection: this is the story with which I opened this article. Notable is the emphasis that Morley places on love, and especially on the lack of malice in the advancement of his two ideal masters: he sees them as humble, fair critics. each willing to give and acceept "censure of that which they had done." We know already from Morley's dedication of the *Plaine and Easie Introduction* that Byrd was, if not his actual master, a model of scholarly and musical perfection to which Morley must have aspired during his life.[54] Because Morley saw Byrd as having achieved greatness through the mutual respect and cooperation described above, it is only natural that he would consider such elements to be integral to the proper development of the abilities of musical scholars.

As an example of diligence and dedication to study, Morley references George Waterhouse, who according to his narrative, had surpassed all others in the variety of his setting of the plainsong Miserere:

> my friend and fellow M[aster] *George Waterhouse*, upon the same plainsong of *Miserere*, for varietie surpassed all who ever laboured in that kind of studie. For hee hath alreadie made a thousand waies (yea and though I should talke of halfe as manie more, I should not be farre wide of the truth) everie one different and severall from another. But because I doe hope verie shortlie that the same shall bee published for the benefite of the worlde, and his owne perpetuall glorie, I will cease to speake anie more of them, but onlie to admonish you, that who so will be excellent, must both spend much time in practise, and looke over the dooings of other men.[55]

---

54. The dedication reads, in part: "To these [parents] the prince & (as *Cicero* tearmeth him) the God of the *Philosophers* added our maisters, as those by whose directions the faculties of the reasonable soule be stirred up to enter into contemplation, & searching of more then earthly things: whereby we obtaine a second being, more to be wished and much more durable then that which any man since the worlds creation hath received of his parents: causing us live in the mindes of the vertuous, as it were, deified to the posteritie. The consideration of this hath moved me to publish these labors of mine under your name both to signifie unto the world, my thankfull mind: & also to notifie unto your selfe in some sort the entire love and unfained affection which I beare unto you." Ibid., [p. iii].

55. Ibid., 115.

An upstanding musician will practice and study as Waterhouse did, and occasionally submit his works to the censures of his fellow scholars as did Byrd and Ferrabosco.

Morley similarly takes advantage of his discussion of mensuration to expose the comprehensive knowledge of previous music masters as a worthy goal for ethical scholars, especially in contrast to the slight, superficial knowledge of the contemporary musical community in England:

> Ma[ster:] Those who within these three hundreth yeares have written the Art of Musicke, have set downe the Moodes otherwise then they eyther have been or are taught now in England.
>
> Phi[lomathes:] What have been the occasion of that?
>
> Ma[ster:] Although it bee hard to assigne the cause, yet may we coniecture that although the great musicke maisters who excelled in fore time, no doubt weare wonderfully seen in the knowledge therof, aswell in speciation as practise, yet since their death the knowledge of the arte is decayed and a more slight or superficiall knowledge come in steede thereof, so that it is come now adaies to that, that if they know the common Moode and some *Triples*, they seeke no further.
>
> Phi[lomathes:] Seeing that it is alwaies commendable to know all, I pray you first to declare them as they were set downe by others, and then as they are used now a dayes.[56]

In this example, Morley not only presents the masters of the past as a goal towards which his readers should aspire, but also supports this real ideal through the response of Philomathes, who happens to be the fictional ideal with whom his readers are meant to identify and alongside whom his readers are meant to grow as ethical scholars. Here Morley encourages his readers to echo Philomathes' assertion that "it is alwaies commendable to know all."

Fictional Virtue

As mentioned above, the utilization of the scholar character as a means to model proper ethical behavior is in keeping with the style of the Platonian dialogue: indeed Philomathes, a name which Morley defines in his dedication to *The Triumphes of Oriana* (1601) as "a personage alway desirous, (though in all Arts sufficiently skilfull) to come to a more high perfection or *Summum*

---

56. Ibid., 12.

bonum,"⁵⁷ serves consistently as Morley's fictional scholarly ideal of humility, dedication, and fair musical criticism throughout the treatise. Humility is the first ethical trait that Morley presents to readers through this model student Philomathes, and that virtue appears first in the brief discourse between Philomathes and Polymathes (Philomathes' brother) at the beginning of the treatise, where we see Philomathes humbly admitting his musical ignorance and setting off in search of master Gnorimus in order to correct this error. As the dialogue progresses, Morley immediately reemphasizes and intensifies the presentation of Philomathes' humility, through his opening conversation with Gnorimus. After Philomathes locates the master, he informs him that he has sought him out for a lesson in music. This comes as a great surprise to master Gnorimus, however, as Philomathes had previously spoken out against music, so much so that he was often described by others as a stoic (as mentioned above):

> Phi[lomathes:] My errand is to you, to make myself your scholler. And [...] I am determined not to depart till I have one lesson in Musicke.
>
> Ma[ster:] You tell mee a wonder: for I have heard you so much speake against that art, as to terme it a corrupter of good manners, & an allurement to vices, for which many of your companions termed you a *Stoick*.⁵⁸

Philomathes goes on to admit his previous indiscretion and claim that he now not only acknowledges the importance of music, but is quite eager to learn. He says, "It is true: But I am so farre changed, as of a *Stoick* I would willingly make a *Pythagorian*. And for that I am impacient of delay, I praie you begin even now."⁵⁹ Through this discourse, Morley highlights the proper comportment of an ethical scholar as one who admits his mistakes and humbly devotes himself fully to the true path, even if that means a complete reversal of his philosophical viewpoint. This scene is especially telling in regards to the insufficient masters described in the preface: if they are to gain anything from the *Plaine and Easie Introduction*, then they too must exhibit the same humility and willingness to admit their own insufficiency.

As the conversation continues, Philomathes' scholarly humility is further emphasized, as he admits his ignorance of even basic musical knowledge:

---

57. Morley, *The Triumphes of Oriana*, [p. iii].
58. Morley, *Introduction*, 2.
59. Ibid.

> Ma[ster:] With a good will. But have you learned nothing at all in Musick before?
>
> Phi[lomathes:] Nothing. Therefore I pray begin at the verie beginning, and teach mee as though I were a childe.⁶⁰

There is no musical reason why Philomathes would need to ask to be taught as a child. "Therefore I pray begin at the verie beginning" adequately serves the pedagogical purpose of setting up the starting point for the lesson: if Morley wanted to further promote the treatise, he could have added a line with Philomathes claiming that only master Gnorimus could teach him or that he was the best master and scholar in the land. Instead, this emphasis on beginning at the very beginning with a level of complete submission and reliance on the teacher for both knowledge and instructions on the ethical application of that knowledge helps to demonstrate the ideal student's humble, unassuming approach to learning his art.

Philomathes is not only humble, but he is also dedicated to his education, and, as with humility, Morley emphasizes this element of his character throughout the treatise. In his first discussion with master Gnorimus, we learn that Philomathes is a scholar of obsessive dedication:

> Ma[ster:] I am glad to see you, [Philomathes] seing it is so long agoe since I sawe you, that I thought you had either been dead, or then had vowed perpetually to keepe your chamber and booke, to which you were so much addicted.
>
> Phi[lomathes:] In deede I have beene well affected to my booke.⁶¹

Hyperbole aside, this statement effectively conveys to the reader the high level of commitment that Philomathes gives to his scholarly activities in general, a commitment that Morley would intend his readers to mirror in their own scholarly activities.

The pedagogical and ethical importance of dedication is reinforced again at the end of the first lesson, where Philomathes declares his intention to diligently practice and internalize the principles that master Gnorimus has

---

60. Ibid.

61. Morley, *Introduction*, 2. Here the word addicted does not carry the negative connotations of today, as evidenced by Morley's use of it in the dedication of the *Plaine and Easie Introduction* to describe his admiration for William Byrd: "And so I rest, in all love and affection to you most addicted," Ibid., *Introduction*, [p. iii].

just taught him: "Sir I thanke you, and meane so diligentlie to practise till our nexte meeting, that then I thinke I shall be able to render you a full account of all which you have told me [...]."[62]

Here Philomathes does not mention performance or execution of the knowledge given to him in the first lesson, but rather a "full account," or spoken explanation, of what he has learned. This idea of internalization and understanding is an important element of ethical scholarly development: a good musical scholar should practice the art of music, but also must comprehend the theory behind the practice so that he will be able to discuss musical principles with fellow scholars, justly criticize works that disregard the commonly accepted theories of music, and (more importantly) teach new students once he himself has become a master.

As a final example of Philomathes' addiction to learning, the beginning of the second lesson presents Philomathes' return to master Gnorimus for another lesson, this time on the subject of descant:

> Ma[ster:] What then was the cause of your comming hither at this time?
>
> Phi[lomathes:] Desire to learne, as before.
>
> Ma[ster:] What would you now learne?
>
> Phi[lomathes:] [...] Now sir, I am at this time come to know what Descant is, and to learne the same.
>
> Ma[ster:] I thought you had onely sought to know Pricktsong, whereby to recreate your selfe being wearie of other studies.
>
> Phi[lomathes:] Indeed when I came to you first, I was of that minde: but the common Proverb is in me verified, that *much would have more*: And seeing I have so farre set foote in musicke, I doe not meane to goe backe till I have gone quite through al[l].[63]

Through his bold statement to not leave until he has learned all there is to know about music, Philomathes models the ethical scholarly ideal of dedication not only to one's studies, but to the development of a complete understanding of one's field (which in turn helps to prevent the ignorance and backbiting to which Morley responded so strongly in the introductory material). Here Philomathes also proves that he has heeded his master's advice regarding the emulation of Waterhouse's obsessive reworking of the Miserere plainsong

---

62. Ibid., 55.
63. Ibid., 70.

and is making good on his own statement regarding the necessity of knowing everything about a given subject.

The humility and dedication expressed by Philomathes, and shown in the previous examples, is complemented by the ever important ability to fairly criticize the works of others, which is a theme that returns repeatedly throughout the treatise. Besides the frequent corrections made by the master to his student's work, the first example of fair scholarly criticism on the part of Philomathes appears in the second lesson, when Gnorimus begins to teach him about the theory and practice of fugue. Here Philomathes ventures a criticism of his master's example, based on what he has already been taught about intervals and the character of melodies:

> Phi[lomathes:] If I might play the *zoilus* with you in this example, I might find much matter to cavill at.
>
> Ma[ster:] I pray you let me heare what you can saie against any part of it, for I would be glad that you could not onely spie an oversight, but that you could make one much better.
>
> Phi[lomathes:] First of all, you let the plainsong sing twoe whole notes, for which you sing nothing: secondlie you begin on a sixt.
>
> Ma[ster:] You have the eies of a *Lynx*, in spying faults in my lesson, and I praie God you may bee so circumspect in your owne [...].[64]

The fact that Philomathes waited until the middle of the second lesson to attempt a criticism of his master—and then did so by first asking permission—models the ethical scholarly trait of respect for one's intellectual elders and the tactful presentation of criticism to other scholars. It is true that this first attempt at scholarly criticism smacks of youthful inexperience (what experienced scholar would be brazen enough to claim the ability to find "much matter to cavil at" in the work of their master?), but as the treatise progresses Philomathes becomes decidedly more skilled at offering criticism, both to his master and to others (even going so far as to take the lead in the discussion of his brother Polymathes' descant singing in the third lesson).

Philomathes also considers the opinions of other scholars when making musical criticisms. When master Gnorimus gives him an example of improper discords in the discussion of descant—discords which he claims should be shunned and are the worst of their kind in existence (he goes so far as to say

---

64. Morley, *Introduction*, 76.

that if anyone can find a worse set of discords than these that he will confess to being ignorant of his profession)—he also explains that this mode of making descant has been improperly praised by many in recent years. Instead of taking this statement as a cue from his master to denigrate those individuals who have praised and used this set of dissonances improperly, Philomathes offers credit to those unnamed individuals before expressing his personal opinion: "Phi[lomathes:] It may bee there is art in this which I cannot perceive, but I thinke it goeth but unpleasinglie to the eare, speciallie in the two notes next before the close."[65] By allowing for the possible existence of art that is beyond his perception, Philomathes avoids an outright condemnation of the scholars that have previously praised the example in question, a kindness that unethical scholars certainly would not have extended in the same situation.

In other instances, Philomathes abstains from passing judgment when he feels unqualified to express a personal opinion. This occurs twice during the discussion of the use of dissonances in the singing of descant, first after he presents a sample of his work to master Gnorimus that contains a number of errors, and again after the master describes the use of flats and sharps as a matter for the discretion of each composer: "Phi[lomathes:] It is not for me to judge or censure your workes, for I was far dashed in my laste waye (which I thought so exceeding good) that I dare never credite mine owne judgement hereafter [...] [in the matter of sharps and flats] It is not for me to disallow your opinion [...]."[66] Here Philomathes responds humbly to the realization that his previous exercise was inferior: rather than becoming argumentative and defensive (as an unethical scholar might) by prudently declining to comment on matters that he feels unqualified to form opinions on Philomathes avoids making ignorant statements and unfair criticisms, a characteristic which Morley highlights as a necessity for all ethical scholars.

Morley's Method of Ethical Pedagogy: Real and Fictional Examples of Vice

While the above examples offer Morley's readers the opportunity to learn ethical scholarship alongside Philomathes, they provide only half of a true course in the art, which would require the presentation of contrasting examples of vicious behavior against which scholarly virtue may be highlighted and

---

65. Ibid., 82.
66. Ibid., 88.

framed. Morley must have known as much, for he includes just as many examples (again both real and fictional) of negative scholarly behavior within the dialogue of the *Plaine and Easie Introduction* as he does positive ones.

Real Vice

Turning first to examples that comment on the real world beyond the treatise, Morley voices his displeasure with unfair criticism in the discussion of canon in the second lesson, where he has the master confess that he has gone about explaining meter in a manner, "not according as it ought to bee in reason, but to content wranglers, who I know will at everie little oversight, take occasion to backbite, and detract from that which they cannot disprove."[67] Though spoken by master Gnorimus, the complaint is directly from Morley and references the wranglers within his own musical community who either had already attacked his treatise, or who he believed would have attacked it if his discussion of meter had been framed differently. In any case, Morley makes a clear statement to his readers regarding the wrong way to criticize the work of other scholars. Not only do unethical scholars use "oversight" as an excuse to attack their peers, but they do so without even being able to prove that the errors they perceive are truly incorrect, just as the ignorant asses of the preface condemn others without any reason.

During the same lesson, master Gnorimus admonishes Philomathes not to think too highly of his own work, because of the danger that conceit and arrogance pose for those on the path to excellence:

> Ma[ster:] Conceit of their own sufficiencie hath overthrowne many, who otherwise woulde have proved excellent. Therefore in anie case, never thinke so well of your selfe but let other men praise you, if you bee praise worthie: then may you justlie take it to your selfe, so it bee done with moderation and without arrogancie.[68]

At the end of the lesson, Morley again cautions his reader against following in the footsteps of arrogant, false critics by declaring that their vanity and arrogance inevitably lead to the scorn of the discreet:

> And as for those who stande so much in opinion of their owne sufficiencie, as in respect of themselves they contemn al other men, I wil leave

---

67. Ibid., 90.
68. Ibid., 87.

them to their foolish opinions: beeing assured that everie man but of meane discretion, will laugh them to scorne as fooles: imagining that all the guiftes of God should die in themselves, if they shoulde bee taken out of the worlde.[69]

Here Morley references discretion as a means to entice his readers to support his assessment; if his readers want to be considered men of discretion, then they cannot help but agree.

Conceit appears again in the third lesson, where master Gnorimus and his students are weighing the merits of repeating a plainsong melody twice in a single descant. Here Morley claims that conceit can go beyond the unpleasant reflection of arrogance to conscious attempts to deceive others:

> [Master:] and though a man (conceiting himselfe in his own skil, & glorying in that he can deceive the hearer) should at the first sight sing such a one as this is, yet another standing by, and perchance a better musicion then he, not knowing his determination and hearing that unpleasantnesse of the musicke might justly condemne it as offensive to the eare.[70]

From the frequent appearance and condemnation of the scholarly vice of conceit, which is commented upon more often than any other scholarly vice throughout the treatise, it appears to have held considerable importance for Morley. Conceit is, after all, the antithesis of humility, which was the first scholarly virtue modeled by Philomathes at the beginning of the treatise.

Laziness too can stem from an individual's belief that their understanding and abilities are unsurpassable, and such a vice stands in direct contrast to the virtue of dedication that Morley so often returned to throughout the book. The inability to accept criticism and the practice of giving unfair criticism also stem from conceit, for the arrogance of unethical scholars prevents them from comprehending the inferiority of their own works and opinions, which results in feelings of jealousy and attacks on the works of others.

Finally, in the discussion of musical genres during the third lesson of the treatise, Morley highlights the general bitterness and proclivity for false criticism of the English community, by contrasting it with the love and consideration of the Italian musical community. Morley first exposes this contrast

---

69. Ibid., 115.
70. Ibid., 124.

through the voice of master Gnorimus, whose role as a master character again lends credibility to the account. Morley further emphasizes this point by reiterating Gnorimus' statement through his student Polymathes (the more academically experienced of the two students):

> [Master:] so much bee they [Italians] by nature inclined to love, and therein are they to be commended for one musicion amongst them will honor and reverence another, whereas by the contrarie, we (if two of us bee of one profession) will never cease to backbite one another so much as we can.
>
> [Polymathes:] but whereas one musicion amongst them will reverence and love one another, that is in deede praiseworthie, and whereas you justly complaine of the hate and backbiting amongst the musicions of our countrey, that I knowe to bee most true, and speciallie in these young fellowes, who having no more skill then to sing a part of a song perfectlie, and scarselie that [,] will take upon them to censure excellent men, and to backbite them too, but I would not wish to live so long as to see a set of bookes of one of those young yonkers compositions, who are so ready to condemne others.[71]

This presentation of a single focused statement with immediate reiteration is unique in the *Plaine and Easie Introduction* and emphasizes once again the deplorable climate that Morley was attempting to correct with his treatise. Like Dowland's criticism of "young men, professors of the Lute, who vaunt themselves to the disparagement of such as have beene before their time, (wherein I my selfe am a party) that there never was the like of them,"[72] Morley's reference here to "young yonkers" further suggests that the infighting in the musical community was the result of tension between older, established musicians, such as Morley and Dowland, and younger, struggling musicians who hoped to supplant the older generation, in part by denigrating them.

Fictional Vice

In addition to the real examples of negative scholarly action presented above, Morley incorporated Philomathes' brother Polymathes and his experience

---

71. Morley, *Introduction*, 150. Morley may have developed his appreciation for the generosity of the Italians as a result of his close associations with Alfonso Ferabosco. Not only does he mention him fondly in relation to Byrd, and praise his music elsewhere in the treatise, but he also gives him pride of place and quantity in his *Madrigals to Five Voyces* (1598), where Ferabosco's madrigals are presented in greater number than those of any other composer and where they also begin and end the collection.

72. John Dowland, *A Pilgrimes Solace*, [p. iv].

with musical instruction into the plot of the dialogue, as a means of further emphasizing the dangers of unethical scholarship and the methods by which the damages of such scholarship might be repaired. Polymathes[73] had previously studied with a master named Boulde, who taught him a number of bad musical and ethical habits and behaved frequently in a manner quite unbecoming of a scholar, let alone a master. The damage done to Polymathes' musical and scholarly manner is eventually repaired, however, and for the remainder of the treatise Polymathes takes his place alongside his brother as an exemplary pupil of master Gnorimus.[73] Unlike Philomathes, Polymathes is described as already having received some training in music at the time of his introduction to Gnorimus, but much of what he learned had been forgotten through inactivity: "Pol[ymathes:] I could have both song [sic.] upon a plainsong, and beganne to set three or foure parts, but to no purpose, because I was taken from it by other studies, so that I have forgotten those rules which I had [been] given me for setting."[74] Furthermore, before joining his brother as a student of Gnorimus, Polymathes' behavior was quite unethical:

> [Philomathes:] ... I have a Brother a great scholler, and a reasonable musition for singing: he, at my first comming to you conceived an opinion (I know not upon what reason grounded,) that I should never come to any meane knowledge in musicke; and therefore, when he heard me practise alone, he would continually mock me; indeede not without reason, for many times I would sing halfe a note too high, other while as much too lowe; so that he could not conteyne himselfe from laughing: yet now and then he would set me right, more to let mee see that he could doe it, then that he meant any way to instruct me: which caused me so diligently to apply my pricksong booke; that in a manner, I did no other thing but sing practising, to skip from one key to another, from flat to sharp, from sharp to flat, from any one place in the Scale to another, so that there was no song so hard, but I would venture upon it, no Mood nor Proportion so strange, but I would goe through and sing perfectly before I left it: and in the ende I came to such perfection, that I might have been my brothers maister: for although he had a little more practise to sing at first sight then I had: yet for the Moods Ligatures, and other such things I might set him to schoole.[75]

---

73. Morley may have chosen Polymathes' name as a means to emphasize the fact that Polymathes is more experienced and more learned than his brother, but ends up falling behind him because of his bad habits. It might also be a means to indicate that those who love learning are naturally better off than those who are simply skilled in multiple disciplines.

74. Morley, *Introduction*, 117.

75. Ibid., 69–70.

Polymathes' loss of ability through a lack of dedication shows the danger of laziness and contrasts sharply with the model of humility and fair criticism set forth by Philomathes: Polymathes' ethical failings are demonstrated by his deciding to help his brother out of arrogance, his unjust opinion that his brother will never be proficient at music, and his discourteous mocking. Because of his ethical scholarly behaviour, however, Philomathes is able to rise above his unethical brother and attain a level of skill that not only makes him technically superior, but perhaps even his "brothers maister."

This master/student relationship appears again when Polymathes follows his brother to the third lesson; the lesson begins when master Gnorimus asks Polymathes to sing an example of descant as a means by which to judge his skill and the skill of his previous master Boulde, and the passage that follows marks a significant turning point in the interaction of the characters within the dialogue. According to the precedent established by the previous two-thirds of the work, one would expect master Gnorimus to constructively criticize Polymathes' example and thereby instruct him on how to improve his descanting ability. This passage breaks with Morley's previous precedent, however, when master Gnorimus abstains from commenting on Polymathes' performance and leaves the task of scholarly criticism to Philomathes, interjecting only once to ask Philomathes to explain his rationale for disliking Polymathes' descant. Not only does Morley give Philomathes the lead role in critiquing Polymathes' descant, but he also ends the discussion of Polymathes' first example of descant without any criticism or educational discourse from master Gnorimus, thereby temporarily allowing Philomathes to act as a master figure, and highlighting Philomathes' personal growth as a scholar with sufficient knowledge and ethics to instruct his scholarly peer (one who just happens to have more experience, but cannot advance because of his unethical habits). If Morley had not added Polymathes to the dialogue, it would have been impossible to place Philomathes in this position of authority, as it would be highly irregular for a student to attempt to correct (rather than criticize) his master, as a peer or otherwise.

This example also gives readers the first glimpse of master Boulde's musical style, which is severely lax when compared to the style espoused by master Gnorimus:

Ma[ster:] Who taught you?

Pol[ymathes:] One maister *Boulde*.

Ma[ster:] I have heard much talke of that man, and because I would know the tree by the fruit, I pray you let me heare you sing a lesson of discant.

Pol[ymathes:] I wil[l] [...]

[Gnorimus provides a simple plainsong, and Polymathes descants upon it]

Phi[lomathes:] Brother if your discanting bee no better then that, you will gaine but small credit by it.

Pol[ymathes:] I was so taught, and this kind of discanting was by my maister allowed, and esteemed as the best of all descant.

Phi[lomathes:] Who ever gave him his name hath either foreknown his destinie, or then hath well and perfectlie read *Plato* his *Cratylus*.[76]

Pol[ymathes:] Why so?

Phi[lomathes:] Because there bee such bolde taking of alowances as I durst not have taken if I had feared my maisters displeasure.

Ma[ster:] Why wherein do you disallow them?

Phi[lomathes:] First of all in the second note is taken a discord for the first part of the note, and not in the best manner nor in binding: the like faulte is in the fifth note, and as for the two notes before the close, the end of the first is a discord to the ground, and the beginning of the next likewise a discord, but I remember when I was practising with you, you did set me a close thus, which you did so farre condemne as that (as you saide) there could not readily bee a worse made, and though my brothers bee not the verie same, yet is it Cosin germaine to it, for this descendeth where his ascendeth, and his descendeth where this ascendeth, that in affect they be both one.

Pol[ymathes:] Do you then find fault with the first part of the second note.

Phi[lomathes:] Yea, and justly.

Pol[ymathes:] It is the fuge of the plainsong, and the point will excuse the harshnesse, and so likewise in the fift note, for so my maister taught me.

Phi[lomathes:] But I was taught otherwise, and rather then I would have committed so grosse oversighis [oversights] I would have left out the point, although here both the point might have beene drought [brought] in otherwise, and those offences left out.

Ma[ster:] I pray you (good master *Polymathes*) sing an other lesson.[77]

---

76. Morley is alluding here to the topic of Plato's *Cratylus*, which is a dialogue on the nature of names and whether or not they are arbitrary or carry some inherent connection to the things that they identify. The point here is that Boulde's name fits his personality and thereby represents an inherent connection between the word and the character of the individual to which it was assigned.

77. Morley, *Introduction*, 117–18.

After two more examples from Polymathes, it becomes clear to master Gnorimus that his new student's musical education has been incomplete so far, which leads the master to ask Polymathes for a description of his previous master and the manner of his musical instruction. What follows is one of the most vividly unflattering descriptions of an ignorant, arrogant, and unethical scholar that Morley could have devised:

> Phi. [Polymathes, improperly marked as Phi. in the original:] when I learned descant of my maister *Bould*, hee [...] would sing the plainsong, and cause me sing the descant, and when I song not to his contentment, he would shew me wherein I had erred, there was also another descanter, a companion of my maisters, who never came in my maisters companie (though they weare much conversant together) but they fel to contention, striving who should bring in the point soonest, and make hardest proportions, so that they thought they had won great glorie if they had brought in a point sooner, or sung harder proportions the one then the other: but it was a worlde to heare them wrangle, everie one defending his owne for the best. What? (saith the one) you keepe not time in your proportions, you sing them false (saith the other) what proportion is this? (saith hee) *Sesquipaltery* saith the other, nay (would the other say) you sing you know not what, it should seeme you came latelie from a barber's shop [...]. so that if one unacquainted with musicke had stood in a corner and heard them, he would have sworne they had beene out of their wittes, so earnestlie did they wrangle for a trifle, and in truth I my selfe have thought sometime that they would have gone to round buffets with the matter, for the descant bookes were made *Angels*, but yet fistes were no visiters of eares, and therefore all parted friendes: but to say the very truth, this *Poliphemus* had a verie good sight, (speciallie for treble descant) but very bad utterance, for that his voice his voice [sic] was the worst that ever I heard, and though of others he were esteemed verie good in that kinde, yet did none thinke better of him then hee did of himselfe, for if one had named and asked his opinion of the best composers living at this time, hee woulde say in a vaine glory of his owne sufficiencie
>
> [...]
>
> Pol[ymathes:] This *Polyphemus* carrying such name for descant, I thought it best to imitate him, so that every lesson which I made was a counterfet of som of his, for at all times and at every occasion I would foist in some of his points which I had so perfectly in my head as my *pater noster*, and because my maister himselfe did not dislike that course I continued still therein, but what saide I? dislike it hee did so much like it as ever where he knewe or found any such example he would wright it out for me to imitate it.[78]

---

78. Ibid., 120–21.

This passage serves as much as a cautionary portrait of an unethical master as it does a criticism of the behavior that both the master Boulde character and his associate Polyphemus exemplify. These men are obsessed with their own abilities, even though they are deemed inferior by Polymathes, and they often fight amongst themselves over which one is the best at singing descant. Furthermore, their insistence on the superiority of their own work over the works of others brands them as unethical scholars, ones who exemplify the unethical behaviors of conceit, ignorance, and unfair criticism. These were all significant scholarly vices that Morley had been careful to caution his readers against previously.

While the discussion of master Boulde and his associate Polyphemus would seem to be superfluous from the standpoint of musical pedagogy, from the perspective of ethical pedagogy the examples that include them are invaluable. As named characters, these individuals personify the numerous criticisms made by Morley against scholarly vice, and, by presenting them as villains, Morley makes it clear to his readers that they are not to be emulated. In fact, Morley may have made the decision to give Boulde an English name rather than a Greek one to make sure that his readers would understand that Polymathes' former master is meant as the ultimate negative example of the treatise. Polyphemus may be just as bad as Boulde, of course, but Boulde does the most harm by leading an innocent scholar down the path to vice. These examples of unethical scholarly activity, therefore, complete the framework of ethical pedagogy, enhancing and emphasizing the good examples of Philomathes and Polymathes: just as master Gnorimus provides examples of incorrect musical passages in order to reinforce the correct use of dissonances, so too does Morley give his readers examples of unethical scholarly behavior in order to reinforce the positive examples of scholarly ethics presented by his real and fictional scholarly ideals.

Conclusion

If teaching the theory and practice of music had been Morley's sole pedagogical goal in writing the *Plaine and Easie Introduction*, then a number of elements within the work would appear to be superfluous. For example, the addition of Polymathes to the dialogue (especially so late in the work), the presentation of the manner by which his master taught him, and the lengthy discussion of the unethical character of both Boulde and Polyphemus would have served little pedagogical purpose in a discussion of music that had been crafted without consideration for the pedagogy of ethical scholarship. Also, the frequent mention of the dangers of conceit and the emphasis on proper scholarly criticism would have served no musical purpose in a work written without regard for scholarly ethics. Certainly none of the authors of 16th-century music theory and practical music texts in England interrupted the flow of their methods to comment on ignorance and arrogance in a manner even close to Morley's.

It might be argued, however, that the above features serve to enhance the dramatic interest and selling power of the work, and that the ethical influence that they exert on the reader is merely an unintentional byproduct. One piece of evidence that refutes this argument, however, is Morley's unusual choice of the Platonian style over the Ciceronian. If the non-musical elements of the *Plaine and Easie Introduction* were meant as commercial enhancements only, then the choice of a dialogical style that was uncommon for music texts in a country that had no discernible interest in dialogical discussions of music to begin with, combined with a failure to take advantage of the craze in Morley's England for Italian music that the overtly Italian Ciceronian style could have played into, would have been a glaring oversight for an author with a mind for commercial success. Furthermore, the emphasis that Morley places on unethical scholarship, and the passion with which he addresses it in his introduction and conclusion is telling of overwhelming frustration, and if he did not consciously intend the work to serve a dual purpose, it nevertheless developed into one as a result of his fixation on the inescapable social atmosphere of his time.

Bibliography

Contemporary Sources

Baynes, Roger. *The Prayse of Solitarinesse.* London: Francis Coldocke and Henry Bynneman, 1577. Available on *Early English Books Online.*

Bevin, Elway. *A Briefe and Short Instruction of the Art of Musicke.* London: R. Young, 1631. Reprinted in *Music Theory in Britain, 1500–1700: Critical Editions*, ed. Denis Collins. Aldershot and Burlington, VT: Ashgate, 2007.

Byrd, William. *A Gratification unto Master John Case, for his Learned Book, Lately made in the Praise of Musicke.* [London: 1586 or 1589]. Reprinted in *The Byrd Edition*, vol. 16, ed. Philip Brett. London : Stainer and Bell, 1978. Also see *The English Poetry Full-Text Database.* Cambridge, England: Chadwyck-Healey, 1994. Also available on *Early English Books Online.*

Case, John. *The Praise of Musicke.* Oxford: Joseph Barnes, 1586. Reprinted in *Anglistica and Americana.* New York: G. Olms, 1980. Also available on *Early English Books Online.*

Campion, Thomas. *A New Way of Making Fowre Parts in Counterpoint.* [Circa 1613]. Reprinted in *Music Theory in Britain, 1500–1700: Critical Editions*, ed. Christopher R. Wilson. Aldershot and Burlington, VT: Ashgate, 2003.

Dowland, John. *The Third and Last Booke of Songs.* London: Thomas Adams, 1603. Reprinted in *The English Lute-Songs*, series I, ed. Edmund Fellowes. London: Stainter & Bell, 1970. Also available on *Early English Books Online.*

———. *A Pilgrimes Solace.* London: J. B. and T. S., 1612. Reprinted in *The English Lute-Songs*, series I, ed. Edmund Fellowes. London: Stainter & Bell, 1970. Also available on *Early English Books Online.*

Erasmus, Desiderius. *Two Dyaloges Wrytten in Laten by the Famous Clerke, D.Erasm[us] of Roterodame, one Called Polyphemus or the Gospeller, the other Dysposyng of Thynges and Names.* Translated by Edmonde Becke. Canterbury: John Mychell, 1550. Reprinted in *Tudor Translations of the Colloquies of Erasmus (1536–1584);* reproductions, edited and with an introd. by Dickie A. Spurgeon. Delmar, NY,1972. Also available on *Early English Books Online.*

Farmer, John. *The First Set of English Madrigals.* London: William Barley, 1599. Reprinted by Da Capo, 1973. Also available on *Early English Books Online.*

Gosson, Stephan. *The Schoole of Abuse.* London: Thomas Woodcocke, 1587. Reprinted by Garland, 1973. Also Available on *Early English Books Online.*

James VI and I, King. *Daemonologie in Forme of a Dialogue*. Edinburgh: Robert Waldegrave, 1597. Reprinted by Da Capo, 1969. Also available on *Early English Books Online*.

Jones, Robert. *The Second Booke of Songs and Ayres*. London: Selman, 1601. Edited by David Greer. Scolar Press, 1971. Also available on *Early English Books Online*.

———. *A Musicall Dreame*. London: Waterson, 1609. Reprinted by Stainer & Bell, 1927. Also available on *Early English Books Online*.

Kirbye, George. *The First Set of English Madrigals*. London: Thomas Easte, 1597. Available on *Early English Books Online*.

Littleton, Sir Thomas. *Tenures in Englishe*. London: Rychard Tottyl, 1576.

Lodge, Thomas. *Protogenes Can Know Apelles*. London: [Singleton], 1579. Available on *Early English Books Online*.

Morley, Thomas. *A Plaine and Easie Introduction to Practicall Musicke*. London: Peter Short, 1597. Facsimile edition: Farnborough: Gregg, 1971.

———. *A Plain & Easy Introduction to Practical Music*, edited by R. Alec Harman. London and New York: Dent, 1952, reprinted 1963.

———, ed.. *The Triumphes of Oriana*. London: Thomas Easte, 1601. Modern edition, London: Stainer & Bell, 1969. Also available on *Early English Books Online*.

Robinson, Thomas. *The Schoole of Musicke*. London: Easte, 1603. Edited by David Lumsden. Paris: CNRS, 1971.

Stubs, Philip. *The Anatomie of Abuses*. London: Richard Johnes, 1595. Reprinted by Garland, 1973. Also available on *Early English Books Online*.

Weelkes, Thomas. *Balletts and Madrigals*. London: Thomas Easte, 1598. Reprinted by Stainer & Bell, 1968. Also available on *Early English Books Online*.

Modern Literature

Buranello, Robert. "From the *Locus Amoenus* to the *Locus Ambiguus*: Sperone Speroni and the Setting of Renaissance Dialogue." PhD diss., University of Toronto, 1999.

Harmon, Roger. "From Themistocles to Philomathes: 'Amousos' and 'Amousia' in Antiquity and the Early Modern World." *International Journal of the Classical Tradition* 9 (2003), 351–90.

Herissone, Rebecca. *Music Theory in Seventeenth-Century England*. New York: Oxford University Press, 2000.

Judd, Cristle Collins. "Music in Dialogue: Conversational, Literary, and Didactic Discourse About Music in the Renaissance." *Journal of Music Theory* 52 (Spring, 2008), 41–74.

Leaver, Robin A. *Luther's Liturgical Music: Principles and Implications*. Grand Rapids, MI: Eerdmans, 2007.

Marsh, Christopher. *Music and Society in Early Modern England*. New York: Cambridge University Press, 2010.

Murray, Tessa. *Thomas Morley: Elizabethan Music Publisher*. Woodbridge: Boydell, 2014.

Owens, Jessie Ann. "You Can Tell a Book by its Cover: Reflections on Format in English Music 'Theory.'" *Music Education in the Middle Ages and the Renaissance*, edited by Susan Forscher Weiss, Russell E. Murray, Jr., and Cynthia J. Cyrus, 347–385. Bloomington: Indiana University Press, 2010.

Stainer, Sir John. "Morley's *Plaine and Easie Introduction to Practicall Musicke*." *The Musical Times and Singing Class Circular* 43 (1 July, 1902), 457–60.

Stern, David. "Thomas Morley and The Teaching of Modal Composition in the Renaissance." *Theoria: Historical Aspects of Music Theory* 17, (2010), 59–112.

Strang, C. "Tripartite souls, Ancient and Modern: Plato and Sheldon." *Apeiron: A Journal for Ancient Philosophy and Science* 16, no. 1 (June, 1982), 1–11.

Vives, Juan Luis. "Princeps Puer." In *Tudor School-Boy Life*, ed. and trans. Foster Watson, 172–84. London: Cass, 1908.

Weiss, Susan, et al. *Music Education in the Middle Ages and Renaissance*. Bloomington: Indiana University Press, 2010.

Wilson, K. J. *Incomplete Fictions: The Formation of English Renaissance Dialogue*. Washington, D.C.: Catholic University of America, 1985.

TONAL SPACE ORGANIZATION IN JOSQUIN'S LATE MOTETS*

DANIELE SABAINO AND MARCO MANGANI

Some years ago, in a paper read at the International Musicological Society Zürich Congress and published the following year in *Acta Musicologica*, we proposed a re-thinking of the concept of tonal type as a hermeneutical tool in the organisation of tonal space of (late) Renaissance polyphony.[1] Our starting point—founded upon a critical reading of the musicological literature on the topic, but also formed around a conviction that seems to us every day more and more reasonable[2]—was the idea that it was unlikely that a sixteenth-century musician could be about to compose a polyphonic piece without any previous concept of tonal space (coincident or not with the traditional concept of plainchant modality, of which we can take almost for granted he had knowledge).[3]

Such a conviction, it should be remembered, reopens the question of the relevance of the concept of mode for the analysis of Renaissance polyphony, for which Harold Powers' studies seemed to have led to a largely negative view.[4] According to those studies, in fact, before attempting any hypothesis about the possible modal categories to which to assign a polyphonic piece, it is imperative to adopt an etic approach and consider the repertoire using three classification tools called by Harold Powers "minimal markers." They are:

(1) the system: that is whether the composition was set in the 'b-natural system' with no signature (called *cantus durus*) or the 'b-flat system' with a b-flat signature (called *cantus mollis*);

---

* An abridged version of this article was presented at the 19th Congress of the International Musicological Society "Musics–Cultures–Identities" held in Rome from the 1st to the 7th July, 2012. In preparing the article, Daniele Sabaino dealt with the analysis of chant-based compositions, Marco Mangani with the analysis of free-composed motets; both authors are responsible for the introduction and the conclusions.

1. Mangani and Sabaino, "Tonal types and modal attribution."
2. In itself, and especially when compared with divergent ideas.
3. Judd, "Renaissance modal theory," 367–77.
4. See, at least, the following papers by Powers: "Tonal Types and Modal Categories"; "Modal Representation," and "Anomalous Modalities."

(2) the overall vocal *ambitus*, expressed by "the choice of one or the other of two ever more standardized combinations of clefs, the so-called "chiavette" and the 'standard' clefs,"[5] resulting normally in a *cantus* set in g_2 and c_1 clef respectively; and

(3) the final sonority of the composition, articulated by the pitch-class of its last lowest note.

In such a manner, for example, the minimal marker combination "♭–g2–F" describes a piece where the B-pitch class is flat, the voices have a high compass (the standard combination of clefs being g_2 for the Cantus, c_2 for the Altus, c_3 for the Tenor, and f_4 or f_3 for the Bassus), and the last sonority has an F as a lower note. If all the possible combinations of the three minimal markers are taken into account, twenty-four "tonal types" result,[6] a far larger number than the eight categories of the chant tradition or the twelve of Glarean's re-thinking of the medieval system. Sometimes, thanks to the existence of modally ordered collections of motets or madrigals, one can discern that the tonal types had a modal meaning also for the composers. The core of Powers' reflection, however, is that it can be argued

> that in given instances a tonal type may be intended to *represent* a mode in a categorical scheme; that is not to say, though, that the tonal type in question is that mode. The distinction is what an anthropologist of music might call a distinction between 'etic' and 'emic.' A tonal type is minimally identifiable by its three markers and thus objectively observable completely apart from its musical or cultural context; it is 'scientific,' it is 'etic.' 'Mode' conversely is all bound up in sixteenth-century musical culture, not only as a living doctrine of the music of the church and a heritage from the Middle Ages but also as a musical construct being experimented with by members of the culture, from both humanistic and traditional points of view; it is thoroughly 'emic' and requires study on its own terms, as well as in relation to any music with which it may be connected.[7]

In his later years, Powers would further accentuate his skepticism about the relevance of the very concept of mode, posing the question "Is Mode Real?" as a rhetorical one with an implicit, negative answer.[8]

---

5. Ibid.
6. Ibid., 438.
7. Ibid., 439.
8. Powers, "Is Mode Real?"

A further reflection on the relationships between tonal types and modes in such authors as Palestrina and Lasso led us to note that different tonal types 'represent' modes differently—or, better, they 'resist' modal attributions in different and peculiar ways: and they do this to such an extent that the dialectic relationship between the concept of tonal type and the concept of mode (neither of which can actually be considered 'neutral') appears to be extremely fruitful for analytical purposes.[9]

Saying that the very idea of 'tonal type' is not so plain and unproblematic as it may seem (and is normally supposed to be), because tonal types do not behave univocally with respect to modal representation, is in fact the same as affirming that each tonal type has its own 'problematic nature' in relationship to modal representation. We defined this problematic nature as *the level of deviation that each tonal type shows, in the process of modal representation, from one or more of the elements that all the Renaissance theoretical tradition agrees on considering as the main modal parameters* (i.e. Tenor *ambitus*, cadential plan, and *exordium*). This problematic nature can also be ordered along a three step scale that starts from a grade zero—*unproblematic tonal types*: tonal types whose relationships with the represented modes are absolutely clear–, continues with grade 1—*tonal types of moderate problematic nature*: tonal types whose associations with the represented modes are less clear because of some 'elements of disturbance'–, and culminates with grade 2—*tonal types of severe problematic nature*: tonal types whose possible modal links are absolutely awkward, owing to the fact that they display as many elements 'of modal disturbance' as of 'modal corroboration.'

In Palestrina (the first subject of our investigation) the problematic nature of the tonal types can be grouped as follows:

- grade 0: $\flat$–g_2–G, $\flat$–g_2–F, $\natural$–c_1–G; $\flat$–c_1–G, $\flat$–c_1–F
- grade 1: $\natural$–g_2–D, $\flat$–c_1–D, $\natural$–g_2–G
- grade 2: $\natural$–g_2–C, $\natural$–g_2–A, $\natural$–c_1–A, $\flat$–g_2–A

Further investigation of various modally and non-modally ordered collections by other composers (above all Lasso and Victoria) led us to the discovery that the order of these problematic natures does not seem to depend on the personal choices or preferences of the composer, but—at least in late

---

9. Mangani and Sabaino, "Tonal Types and Modal Attribution"; Sabaino, "Lasso's Motets."

Renaissance polyphony—seems to be inherent to the tonal type itself: in fact, some types are (almost) always problematic, while some others (perhaps more significantly) are (almost) always unproblematic. (This could mean that what Bernhard Meier, in his fundamental study of modes in classical vocal polyphony,[10] viewed as a coherent and balanced organism, rather than a proper system in which *tout se tient*, should perhaps be considered as a collection of different ways of organising the tonal space, each of which has its own peculiarities and its own idiosyncrasies—a suspicion that could be reinforced by the very different ways each mode—and the related psalm tone—evolved into the organization of the modern harmonic tonality.[11] This hypothesis, however, exceeds the boundaries of this essay and deserves further investigation elsewhere).

What we believe our analyses seem to suggest, then, is that the scepticism about the 'reality' of the modal categories which has pervaded musicology in the last decades appears in need of some reconsideration. The famous Powersian question *Is mode real?*,[12] in other words, should not be considered any longer a rhetorical question with an implicit, negative answer. Instead, it must be regarded as a true epistemological question, and reformulated as *In what way and to what extent is mode real?* without any risk of entering a sort of ultra-Meierian *naïveté* and without any need to dismiss the very idea of tonal type.

However, can what appears to work in *late* Renaissance polyphony be said to be—totally? partially?—valid also for *early* Renaissance music? To test the productivity of our new hermeneutical tool in that area, we have turned to the music of Josquin, and analysed some of his late motets.[13] While, in the examination of music by Palestrina and Lasso, we compared modally and non-modally ordered collections (to be able to take into account the same tonal type from an *etic* point of view as well as in the composer's, or publisher's, consideration), in the examination of Josquin's motets we proceeded to

---

10. Meier, *Die Tonarten*; Meier, *Alte Tonarten*.

11. See for example Powers, "From Psalmody to Tonality."

12. Powers, "Is Mode Real?" See also Powers, "Modality as a European Cultural Construct."

13. In order to have a more coherent sample, we chose only compositions whose authenticity has—so far—never been questioned or has been confirmed, and which most musicological literature dates to the years of Ferrara and Condé, that is from 1503 to 1521. See Macey and Noble, "Josquin"; Sherr, "Chronology of Josquin's Life and Career"; Finscher, "Four-Voice Motets"; Milsom, "Motets for Five or More Voices"; Fallows, *Josquin*.

analyse separately *cantus firmus*-based and free compositions, with the intent of evaluating

(1) to what extent the presence of a pre-existing chant, whose modal profile is normally thought to be easily recognizable, affects the modal contour of a polyphonic composition;

(2) whether in this music as well some tonal types are more problematic than others—that is, if also in Josquin's music different tonal types resist differently a modal representation; and

(3) whether the relationships between tonal types and modal categories could provide a useful tool for a deeper understanding of the tonal organization (also) of Josquin's music.

The rest of the article will summarise the results of the analysis.

Let us start with the compositions based on *prius facti* chants, listed in Table 1. Five tonal types are to be considered, which will be defined in this section mainly by their *proprietas* (♮ vs. ♭) and last lowest sonority, since cleffing cannot be considered an 'objective' marker or the same rank (because—not uncommonly—it may be different in different sources[14]). These tonal types are: ♭–D, ♭–F, ♮–G, ♭–G, and ♮–A (only ♭–G, in any case, presents motets either in natural or in high clefs; compositions in the other tonal types are all written in natural clefs.)

1. Three motets belongs to the type ♭–G: the five-voice *Virgo salutiferi* (no. 35, NJE 25.13),[15] the six-voice *O virgo prudentissima* (no. 45, NJE 24.10, not to be confused with *Virgo prudentissima* for four-voices, no. 25, NJE 25.12), and the five-voice *Salve regina* (no. 48, NJE 25.4, the one in *chiavette*).

The last two are absolutely unproblematic as far as modal representation is concerned. *Salve regina* paraphrases the well-known mode 1 chant, and uses its first four notes as a scaffolding motto;[16] *O virgo prudentissima* places in the Tenor the sequence *Beata mater et intacta virgo*, which can easily be assigned to mode 2 because of its limited range (—it does not rise over the fourth above the *finalis* nor descend below the *subfinalis*). For each, the polyphonic setting

---

14. See Molmenti, "L'organizzazione dello spazio sonoro," 128–31.
15. Motet numbers follow *Werken van Josquin des Près, Motetten*. The new number assigned in the New Josquin Edition is also given for each work, after the siglum NJE.
16. For two detailed analyses of this composition, see Judd, "Josquin des Prez: *Salve regina*," and Milsom, "Analysing Josquin."

Table 1. Josquin's *cantus firmus* late motets

Tonal type		Motet	Voices	Werken n° (NJE)	End p. 1	End p. 2	Last Tenor pitch	Notes
♭-D	c1 [c4] c4 c4 f4 f4	*Huc me sydereo*	6 (5?)	32 (21.5)	A	—	A	mensuration *c.f.* in T
	c1 c4 c4 c4 f4 f4	*Ave nobilissima creatura*	6	34 (23.11)	A	—	A	mensuration *c.f.* in T
♭-F	c1 c3 c4 c4 f4	*Inviolata, integra*	5	42 (24.4)	A	A	A	*c.f.* canon at the fifth in T2 and T
♮-G	c1 c3 c4 c4 f4 f4	*Benedicta es*	6	46 (23.13)	G	G	G	*c.f.* canon at the octave in S and T
♭-G	c1 c4 c4 c4 f4	*Virgo salutiferi*	5	35 (25.13)	B♭	C	D	*c.f.* in T2
	c1 c3 c4 c4 f4	*O virgo prudentissima*	6	45 (24.10)	G	—	G	*c.f.* in T
	g2 c3 c3 c3 f3	*Salve regina*	5	48 (25.4)	G	G	D	motto in Q
♮-A	c1 c3 c4 f4	*Miserere mei, Deus*	5	37 (18.3)	E	E	E Tenor 1 A Tenor 2	moving motto in T2

mirrors closely the tonal organisation of its chant, especially in the design of the *exordia* and in the choice of cadential goals.[17]

Salve regina, besides being written in high clefs, cadences almost solely on G and D, and avoids carefully any stop on C (the end of the first half of each motto statement, which in its entirety spans exactly the authentic Dorian octave transposed to G). *O virgo prudentissima* insists even more on the *finalis* G, leaving very little space for other cadential sonorities. The vocal ranges of *O virgo* also reflect precisely theoretical descriptions of the *ambitus* proper to the second mode. In contrast, a wider Superius range, combining almost completely the authentic and the plagal *ambitus* of the G-Dorian species, audibly marks *Salve regina*. However, this wider range does not constitute a problem intrinsic to the modal representation: rather, it stems from a register spacing very typical of Josquin, a high voice set against a group of low ones, resulting in a Superius covering also the Alto range and an Alto and a Tenor sharing nearly the same *ambitus*.[18]

The third motet, *Virgo salutiferi*,[19] when compared with the clarity exhibited by *Salve Regina* and *O virgo prudentissima*, states the mode somewhat less firmly. First, its *cantus prius factus*—the antiphon *Ave Maria*—is unmistakably in mode 1, as the intonation formula makes clear at the very beginning; in the first part of the composition, however, Josquin repeats the melodic portion over "Dominus tecum" at the lower fourth, so giving the Tenor a perfect plagal *ambitus*. Second, all the non-canonic voice ranges are *plusquamperfecti*, destroying the balance of authentic and plagal conventions in adjacent registers. Third, the motet displays—beside cadences on G—more cadences on B♭ (the repercussion of the transposed *second* mode; even the first part of the motet closes on that note) than on D (the repercussion of the transposed first mode): and this not because of any needs arising from *cantus firmus* melodic design or segmentation, but from an unfathomable decision on the part of the composer. Fourth, the second part of the composition ends on C (with a non-cadential termination), again from a deliberate choice by Josquin, since the end of the portion of chant he uses would easily have permitted a more standard ending on

---

17. Appendix 2 of Judd, "Aspects of Tonal Coherence" contains a useful list of "Cadential profiles" of many Josquin's motets.
18. Krantz, "Rhetorical and Structural Functions of Mode," 213. For a different perspective on the motet, see van Benthem, "A Triumph of Symbiosis."
19. For an analysis of the *fuga* in this motet, see Milsom, "Josquin des Prez and the Combinative Impulse."

G.[20] The impression of modal opacity is reinforced by the beginning of the *secunda pars*, which outlines the Lydian, and not the Dorian, species of fifth—it may be that Josquin, by the immediate succession of cadences on F and on G, wanted to emphasize the textual juxtaposition "tu potis es primae scelus expurgare parentis" vs. "humanumque Deo conciliare genus": the F-area, foreign to the mode, would exegetically incarnate the *scelus*, while the G-area would indicate the return to the primeval status of familiarity with the Creator. In any case, a modal tension is at work in this part of the motet, and the perception of its main tonal focus momentarily obscured.

2. Only one late motet is associated with each of the tonal types ♭–F, ♮–G, and ♮–A: the ♭–F five-voice *Inviolata, integra et casta es, Maria* (no. 42, NJE 24.4), the ♮–G six-voice *Benedicta es, caelorum regina* (n. 46, NJE 23.13), and the ♮–A five-voice *Miserere mei Deus* (n. 37, NJE 18.3). The first is a plain and unproblematic composition with regard to modal representation, the second involves some minor problems, while the third needs some special consideration.

Inviolata contains a *cantus firmus* in a patent mode 6 (because of the range, shorter than an octave, and especially because of the weight of the sound A in the melodic contour of the chant). The polyphony conforms to that modal environment by the use of a plagal *ambitus* in both Superius and Tenor, by the quality of the *exordium* (which firmly establishes the octave C–c with a clear division on F), and by the recurrence of cadences on F and on A (these last, which terminate also the first and the second part, are the result of the conclusion of several *cantus firmus* phrases and are, in turn, the major cause of a few cadences on E generated by the flow of the canon at the fifth). From an external point of view,[21] the representation of the sixth mode—in

---

20. According to Judd, "Aspects of Tonal Coherence," 127, the final G at the end of the first two parts of the motet is consciously avoided "to mark the partial nature of the *cantus firmus*" and to reserve the very final to third and last part, "which states the antiphon in its entirety."

21. We use the term 'external' in the sense intended by Frans Wiering in his "Internal and External Views" and *The Language of the Modes* (97–98). It denotes a modal classification of a piece based mainly on the final sonority, regardless of the contour of the melody (or polyphony), the inner cadences and even the range of (the/each) voice (a way of proceeding condensed in the old Medieval dictum *Omnis modus in fine dignoscitur*). It opposes an 'internal view,' which sees the modal assignment of a given composition as the result of an overall consideration of the entire musical development of the piece. The latter view can be said to belong "to musical speculation, the former to musical craftsmanship" (*The Language of the Modes*, 97). Clearly, in their purest form, the two views are almost an abstraction, but in general they are a helpful device for discriminating the different tendencies about modality that can be observed in Renaissance theory and practice (and even to soften the opposition of the seemingly irreconcilable critical positions of Meier and Powers).

the eight-mode system—is confirmed by Zarlino, who quotes the motet as an example of mode 12 in chapter 29 of the fourth part of his Le Istitutioni Harmoniche:[22]

> Tal modo appresso gli ecclesiastici fu poco in uso anticamente: ma li più moderni, con l'aiuto del tetracordo *synemennon* [sic], cioè con la corda b, hanno fatto la maggior parte delle loro cantilene che erano del sesto modo, del modo duodecimo [...] Si trovano di questo modo innumerabili cantilene composte da molti musici prattici, tra le quali è il mottetto *Inviolata, integra et casta est Maria* di Iosquino a cinque [...] voci.[23]

Equally patent is the mode 8 of the *cantus prius factus* in *Benedicta es*. In the polyphony, the voice-range complies with the expectation of the theorists, and the treatment of the *cantus prius factus* reveals Josquin's intention to introduce some caesuras, to correspond with modally significant pitches. The first sentence of the chant text, "Benedicta es, caelorum regina," for instance, is broken after *Benedicta*, and not after *es*, as would have been much more logical, surely in order to escape a phrasal articulation on A. Only the cadential plan shows some discrepancies with respect to the general theoretical framework: there are almost no cadences to C, while there are some to D, the *repercussa* of the paired mode 7 (although the absolute majority of cadences are to the *finalis* G: the note C however—as Steven Krantz has noted[24]—has a pivotal role in the linear organisation of the vocal lines). These discrepancies are reflected in the modal assignments by Glarean and Zarlino: Glarean classifies the motet as Mixolydian (as regards the Tenor): "Sed de ipso nunc exempla referamus [...] Quidam Iosquino adscribunt in cantu quinque vocum *Benedicta es*";[25] Zarlino instead sees it as Hypomixolydian: "Appresso gli altri musici si trovano molte composizioni [dell'ottavo modo], tra le quali si trovano li motetti *Benedicta es coelorum regina* di Iosquino [...] e molti altri

---

22. From here onwards the references will always be to the first, 1558 edition of the book and to its modal numbering. In the second edition, following the publication of the *Dimostrationi Harmoniche*, as is well-known, Zarlino modified the numbering and deviated from the traditional as well as from Glareanian ordering.

23. Zarlino, *Le Istitutioni Harmoniche*, part. IV, ch. 29, 334.

24. Krantz, "Rhetorical and Structural Functions of Mode," 310.

25. Glarean, *Dodecachordon*, lib. III, ch. 22, 346. (The Cantus, according to Glarean, is instead Hypomixolydian; it should be noted, however, that the theorist refers—and not without problems—only to the *secuna pars* of the motet, which he attributes to Mouton, even though he is aware that "Quidam Iusquino adscribunt". See Krantz, "Rhetorical and Structural Functions of Mode," 307, n3.

quasi infiniti."[26] Since the motet is the only one composed by Josquin in this tonal type, it is risky to make generalisations; yet its broad conformation allows us to conclude that its problematic nature is almost identical to that noticed in numerous motets by Palestrina and Lasso that are set out in the same tonal type. Therefore, the ambiguity of modal representation, also in Josquin, seems not to depend on odd compositional choices, but to be intrinsic to the tonal type itself.

The single piece in ♮–A is the famous psalm-motet *Miserere mei Deus*.[27] Its possible modal representation is quite problematic, as is indirectly confirmed by the different attributions given by Aron and Glarean, who assign the composition respectively to the irregular Phrygian[28] and to the (new) Hypoaelian mode.[29] The same motet is a *quaestio disputata* also in many modern discussions, the principal being by Meier, Krantz, and Judd. Meier believes that *Miserere mei* is in the third mode commixt with the first, as he sees for example in the eleventh verse, where the sonority of A, previously closely related to the sonority of E, begins instead to be linked with that of D, exploiting the inherent potential of melodic material that "belongs either to the third or the first mode according to the different kinds of interval species."[30] Krantz thinks that both Zarlino and Glarean are in error in considering A as the *finalis* of the motet: the real *finalis* is in fact E, the sonority which ends the *Tenor primus*, the 'free' voice structurally supporting the motet.[31]

---

26. Zarlino, *Le Istitutioni Harmoniche*, part. IV, ch. 25, 329.

27. For a rhetorical analysis of the motet, see Macey, "Josquin and Musical Rhetoric."

28. "Alcuni altri ancora in A la mi re del terzo troverai, negli quali, essendo in essi el processo conforme, saranno giudicati di esso terzo tuono, come *Miserere mei Deus* di Iosquino": Aron, *Trattato della natura et cognitione di tutti gli tuoni*, ch. 5, fol. cr (on the compositions referred to by Aron in this *Trattato*, see Judd, *Reading Aron Reading Petrucci*; and Judd, *Reading Renaissance Music Theory*, 48–68).

29. . "Nunc eius [= of hypoaelian mode] exempla tractanda sunt. Sed ante omnia ea compositio, quam Iodocus Pratensis super psalmum *Miserere mei Deus* quinque instituit vocibus, palmam obtinet": Glarean, *Dodecachordon*, lib. III, ch. 20, 319.

30. Meier, "The Musica Reservata," 77; see also pp. 84–86.

31. "For istance, there is not just one tenor in this motet. There are two, which the vocal sources identify as 'tenor primus' and 'tenor secondus,' and which I shall call the free tenor and ostinato tenor respectively. The free tenor takes over much of the modal function of a standard tenor that the ostinato tenor cannot assume here, particularly the articulation of cadences. Indeed, the free tenor is the 'tenor primus,' and when its role is considered it will become apparent that the scructure of this motet is fairly typical for mode 3, the authentic Phrygian, at least insofar as structures in this mode can ever be said to be typical. For example, the last note of the free tenor is e', not a. In the *prima pars* the free tenor begins in b an ends on g, in the *secuda pars* it begins on e and ends on b, and in the *tertia pars* it begins on c. All of these pitches are structurally more important in mode 3 than in the Hypoaeolian": Krantz, "Rhetorical and Structural Functions of Mode," 238–59: 240.

Finally, Judd also underlines the importance of the 'free' Tenor, but at the same time she frames the contrast between the two theorists within a broader consideration of their respective approaches, and emphasizes the new directions taken by both treatises:

> These two theorists, publishing treatises twenty years apart and in distinct national traditions, represent different viewpoints and one might argue that to compare the observation of Aron within the eight-mode system of classification and Glarean with his twelve-mode system is simply to compare different things. But their treatises share one crucial feature: both move in new directions with their references to composed polyphony. They represent individual viewpoints in their choice of music examples and it does not appear that the examples were chosen capriciously, but rather with care to supplement the content of the treatises.[32]

Therefore, the global design of the composition raises two fundamental questions: (1) can the last lower sonority A be accounted as a 'true' *finalis?*, and (2) why did Josquin decide to arrest the *Miserere* motto in the second Tenor on A, and not on E (or on B), thereby allowing an E final? The first question should not be confused with the query about an 'internal' vs. 'external' view of the modality of the composition.[33] Even from an 'internal' point of view, in fact (*pace* Krantz), both E and A can claim to be the true modal *finalis*: A because it is the conclusion of the last statement of the quasi-*cantus firmus* motto as well as the goal of the protraction that concludes the motet; E because it is the conclusion of the first Tenor as well as the goal of the last strong (Phrygian) cadence of the work (mm. 415–24: see Example 1).

Rather, the question is about the coincidence or non-coincidence of a 'phenomenological final,' so to speak, and an 'ontological final' (which is a formalised way in which we would like to define what Judd called 'termination' and '*finalis*').[34] Clearly Aron thought of A as only a 'phenomenological' final, while Glarean believed it to be an 'ontological' one. On these bases, the two theorists arrive at their respective assignments: Glarean allots primary importance to the second Tenor and its motto scalar movement, which outlines A as dividing arithmetically the octave E–e and gives way to the

---

32. Judd, "Aspects of Tonal Coherence," 61–66, esp. 64–65.
33. Wiering, "Internal and External Views" and above, n22.
34. Judd, "Aspects of Tonal Coherence," 162–63. Instead, the terminology used here was first introduced in Mangani, *L'organizzazione dello spazio sonoro*.

Example 1. Josquin, *Miserere mei, Deus*, mm. 415–24.

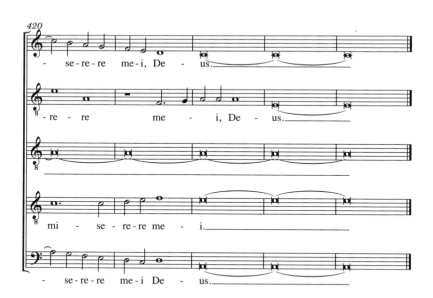

plagal definition of the entire polyphonic building.[35] Aron awards instead prominence to the robust Phrygian *exordium*, which—combined with the range of each voice and the consideration of E as 'ontological' final[36]—points towards the authentic declination of the *deuterus maneries*: a reading we subscribe to more confidently than to Glarean's interpretation. The second question (why Josquin arrested the *Miserere* motto on A, and not on E or on B as the fifth of a Bass E) is more subtle, and obviously any solution can only be as a result of speculation. As Krantz wrote, it could hypothetically be a way of leaving the text supplication open, ending the motet with a deceptive cadence.[37] However, following Meier and the same Krantz, who saw a *commixtio* of Phrygian and Dorian elements in various sections of the composition (Meier even defined the total progression of the work as a *reservata* development "a Dorio ad Phrygium"),[38] it is also possible to think of A as the 'middle term' between E and D, and therefore that the 'phenomenological' final—as happens frequently in many other sixteenth-century compositions we have studied elsewhere[39]—is the best way to draw to a satisfactory conclusion a pervasive inner conflict between Dorian and Phrygian areas, ingeniously interspersed for both rhetorical and expressive purposes.

This highly problematic nature with respect to modal representation also affects the two six-voice motets in ♭-D, *Huc me sydereo* (no. 32, NJE 21.5), where the *Altus prima vox* is possibly spurious[40]) and *Ave nobilissima creatura* (no. 34, NJE 23.11). The motets are twins also because they share the same *cantus firmus* melody[41] (*Ave nobilissima* with the Marian text *Benedicta tu*, and *Huc me* with the Passion text *Plangent eum*),[42] and because the last note of

---

35. Glarean, *Dodecachordon*, lib. III, ch. 20, 320: "Vides nimirum hic Hypoaeolium ex e parvo in E magnum, mediatum quidem arithmetic. in parvo, ubi et finitur, nempe infima diapente chorda, supra autem annexum semitonium. quod ad Principem huius Modi Aeolium vere attinet, sed usurpat et hic eius Plagius."

36. Aron, *Trattato della natura et cognitione di tutti gli tuoni*, fol cr: "essendo in essi el processo conforme."

37. Krantz, "Rhetorical and Structural Functions of Mode," 246.

38. Krantz, "Rhetorical and Structural Functions of Mode," 252–53; Meier, "The Musica Reservata," 77.

39. Mangani and Sabaino, "*Modo Novo or Modo Antichissimo?*"

40. Rifkin, "Motivik—Konstruktion—Humanismus," 106–10.

41. Elders, "*Zusammenhänge.*"

42. The two antiphons are registered in *Corpus Antiphonalium Officii*, vol. 2, *Manuscripti cursus monasticus*, num. 1709 and 4295 respectively.

both *cantus firmi* (A, held by the Tenor) is embedded in a A-sonority at the end of the *prima pars* (reached without any cadential *clausula*), and in a D-sonority at the end of the *secunda pars* (achieved with a proper cadence not resulting from a prolongation). Modal interpretation is very complex, since the *cantus prius factus* is already ambiguous in its modal substance: in the medieval tradition (for example in Worcester F 160[43]), the same basic antiphon model may or may not present B♭ during the course of the chant and before the *finalis* (while Josquin used B♭ throughout the line), with different modal implications (see Example 2).

Depending on how many B♭s are used, the antiphon could assume a Mixolydian (with all or mostly B♮) or a Dorian flavour (with B♭), in both cases with a feeble Phrygian ending. This means that, especially in polyphonic practice, the chant can be read either in the *durus* or in the *mollis* hexachord (*ut re fa sol sol* … or *re mi sol la la*); given the presence of a flat signature, the latter reading seems to be preferred in Josquin's Tenors, even raising the question of the possible *fa supra la* for the highest E (over "*mulieribus*"). This is a possibility that counterpoint only rules out in the last statement of the second part of *Huc me sydereo* (at m. 247), leaving all the other statements of the motet (and all the parallel statements in *Ave nobilissima creatura*) open to the flattening of the high E, with all its accompanying Dorian implications (as in Example 3).

The assignment of the antiphon(s) to the fourth mode, thus, is just a matter of convenience, as it were, as is openly stated by a footnote in the modern *Antiphonale Monasticum*:

> Adsunt quaedam Antiphonae speciales omnes ejusdem typi, vg. *Benedicta* […] quae intra Modorum seriem usu recepta annumerari nullatenus possunt, utpote alteratione cromatica revera insignitae, et inde nullius Modi sunt. Ad fidem tamen codicum, et ratione similitudinis, quae tam in suae clausulae finalis quam in psalmi modulatione viget, quarto Modo de facto assignatae sunt, sed cum nota discretiva 'alterationis.'[44]

Josquin's polyphony appears to assume and amplify the chant ambiguity: the basic ♭–D seems in fact to be used as the middle term between a transposed Dorian (*finalis* G) and a transposed Phrygian (*finalis* A).[45] If this interpretation

---

43. *Antiphonaire monastique*, 13. siècle, 127 (*Plangent eum*) and 268 (*Benedicta tu*).
44. *Antiphonale Monasticum pro diurnis horis*, 1321.
45. Judd, "Aspects of Tonal Coherence," 228 also notes that "the *A mi* final facilitates interaction with *Re* tonality."

Example 2. Josquin, comparison of *cantus firmi* and the related antiphon melodies in Worcester manuscript F.160.

Line 1: the *cantus firmi* of Josquin's *Ave nobilissima creatura* and *Huc me sydereo*; lines 2 and 3: chants from Worcester, ms. F 160 [p. 127 and 268 of *Paléographie Musicale*, vol, 12] .

is correct, D would be a *confinalis* for both G and A, and would work as noted above with regard to the tonal type ♮-A: it is what allows blending the internal tension generated from Dorian and Phrygian basic ingredients (this, incidentally, would favour Zarlino's opinion according to which A-modes—and transposed A-modes—have always existed;[46] something which is true, however, only if we regard those categories not as independent modal entities, as Zarlino pretends, but rather as elegant techniques to connect originally separate sound worlds[47]). Also for this tonal type, then, it is clear that D is not the

---

46. Zarlino, *Le Istitutioni Harmoniche*, part. IV, ch. 26, 329.
47. See Mangani and Sabaino, "Modo Novo or Modo Antichissimo?"

Example 3. Josquin, *Ave nobilissma creatura*, mm. 73–82. From the edition in *Werken van Josquin des Prez*, but in modern clefs.

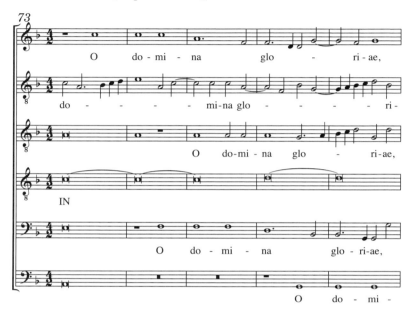

'ontological final' of these motets, but is a purely 'phenomenological' one, albeit necessary for the balance of the system. In the actual music, in fact, the *exordium* is in *re*, and the majority of the cadences are on G: a G, though, which is not to be regarded as *repercussio* of an hypothetical D-Phrygian modality, but as a *finalis* of a ♭-G-Dorian intermingled with a transposed (i.e. with a ♭-A-)Phrygian category. *Huc me sydereo* and *Ave nobilissima creatura*, therefore, cannot be eventually considered purely *deuterus* motets, but should be deemed members of a special class participating in *protus* and *deuterus* modality.

Evidently—as Judd wrote—Josquin's music "was grounded in plainchant,"[48] and the plainchant modality leaves obvious traces on—or better: defines and orients, sometimes patently, sometimes subtly—the tonal organization of the polyphony.[49] Is this compatible with the idea—also advanced by Judd—that "it is unlikely that Josquin thought of himself as composing polyphony in the modes" (even though with the limitation "in the sense of later composers who published modal cycles")?[50] To explore this side of the problem, let us turn to his late free-composed motets.

Josquin's Ferrara and Condé free-composed motets, and those where a pre-existing chant, although present, is not entirely placed in the Tenor, are listed in Table 2. They can be divided into two groups, according to the problematic degree of their respective modal attribution.

No problems, in this sense, seem to subsist in ascribing the low four-voice c_4–♮–E *Domine ne in furore tuo* (no. 39, NJE 16.6) to the third mode, an attribution already advanced "hypothetically"[51] by Judd[52] and which finds us in total agreement. Analogously, the six-voice c_1–♭–G *Pater noster/Ave Maria* (no. 50, NJE 20.9), with its clear-cut canons, shows all the traits of a *protus* transposed *per bemolle* at the higher fourth. Probably conceived as two independent pieces, only later put together as *prima* and *secunda pars*,[53] both the

---

48. Judd, "Aspects of Tonal Coherence," 82.
49. Judd, however, thinks that, even though Josquin "respected the tonal implication of the chant he used," nevertheless "all the evidence suggests that the resulting motet was more often than not divorced from the functional associations of that chant": "Aspects of Tonal Coherence," 127.
50. Judd, "Aspects of Tonal Coherence," 82.
51. Judd, "Aspects of Tonal Coherence," 52.
52. Judd, "Aspects of Tonal Coherence," 53.
53. Freeman, "On the Origins of the *Pater noster–Ave Maria*."

Table 2. Josquin's late motets without *cantus firmus* (in the Tenor)

Tonal type		Motet	Voices	Werken n° (NJE)	End p. I	End p. 2
♮-E	c4 c4 c4 f4	*Domine ne in furore tuo*	4	39 (16.6)	A	—
	cI c3 c4 f3 f4	*De profundis*	5	90 (15.13)	canon at the octave	
♭-F	g2 c3 c3 f3	*In principio erat Verbum*	4	56 (19.8)	D	D
♭-G	cI c3 c3 c4 f4 f4	*Praeter rerum series*	6	33 (24.12)	G	—
	cI c3 c4 c4 c4 f4	*Pater noster / Ave Maria*	6	50 (20.9)	G	—
♮-A	cI c3 c4 f4	*Memor esto verbi tui*	4	3I (17.14)	E	—

freely-composed *Pater* and the following *Ave*, which instead refers to the melody of the Marian antiphon, are altogether contained within the authentic *ambitus*.[54] Even fewer problems are raised by the equally six-voice c_1–♭–G *Praeter rerum seriem* (no. 33, NJE 24.12), that treats the thirteenth-century monophonic sequence almost as a *cantus firmus*, even though with some liberties:[55] as already Zarlino,[56] Eucharius Hoffmann,[57] and Sethus Calvisius[58] have pointed out, we are here facing a easy-to-detect transposed second mode.

The other motets listed in Table 2, on the contrary, present problems of different kinds. We can try to outline a hierarchy, from the motet which seems to be the least problematic up to the most challenging of all the compositions under consideration. The hierarchy, in our opinion, is the following:

---

54. Krantz, "Rhetorical and Structural Functions of Mode," 207–8 recognizes the possible conflicts between the mode of the Marian antiphon of the *secunda pars* (the reciting tone of the *prima pars* "falls into no particular mode") and the mode of the polyphonic building.

55. On the motet and its intabulations see Krantz, "Rhetorical and Structural Functions of Mode," 182–201.

56. Zarlino, *Le Istitutioni Harmoniche*, part. IV, ch. 19, 323: "Si trovano molte compositioni del Secondo modo, composte da molti Antichi, et da Moderni Musici; tra le quali è il motetto, Praeter rerum seriem, composto a sei voci da Iosquino; et da Adriano a Sette voci."

57. Hoffmann, *Doctrina de tonis seu modis musicis*, fol. D3v: "De secundo tono [...] In Figurali, Tulerunt Dominum 8 Vocum Iosquini. Praeter rerum seriem, eiusdem. Veni in hortum, Clementis. Item, Exaudi Domine. Taedet animam meam, Orlandi. Lucerna pedibus meis. Item, Haec est voluntas eius, Galli Dresleri, et cetera."

58. Calvisius, *Exercitationes musicae duae*, 48–49: "Sic et Dorij Remissi sive Hypodorij exempla multa inveniuntur, variora quidem in regulari systemate, longè verò frequentiora in transposito [...] In Transposito systemate [...] Praeter rerum seriem. à 6. Iosquini de Pres."

- *Memor esto verbi tui* (four voices, c_1–♮–A, no. 31, NJE 17.14);
- *In principio erat Verbum* (four voices, g_2–♭–F, no. 56, NJE 19.8);
- *De profundis clamavi ad te, Domine* (five voices, c_1–♮–E, n. 90, NJE 15.13).

Much has been written on *Memor esto* and its astonishing final reprise, in halved values, of the initial motive (not to mention its possible destination as a reminder for King Louis XII).[59] As for the organization of its tonal space, Judd listed this motet among those which would be not classifiable in Aron's terms.[60] Even though Judd might be right about Aron, it must be recalled here that as authoritative a theorist as Glarean found the piece perfectly decipherable in modal terms. Let us briefly reconsider the question.

The main problematic aspect of this motet, which appears to be tonally centered on D from its very beginning, does not reside, as sometimes stated, in its conclusion: as Meier rightly asserted,[61] here we are clearly dealing with a half cadence induced by the word *spem* (hope), which expresses a condition whose further developments are not yet visible. The previous two-voice cadence on D strongly confirms such a hypothesis (Example 4). The real problem is instead the conclusion of the first part of the motet, with a totally unpredictable deviation towards E after an equally clear-cut cadence on D (Example 5).

In this sense, the fact that Glarean's statements about this piece contains a certain criticism of such audacities is not as relevant as it appeared to Meier: far more important is the fact that, for Glarean, the modal outline of the motet was so evident that its deviation from the modal rules ("saepe etiam accidit ut cantus cauda deformetur") could only be perceived as such by the listeners ("Cantores quidam [...] adeo pulchrum existimant Cantuum fines alio torquere, et auditorem suspendere naso").[62] According to such a perspective, then, *Memor esto* appears to be less modally problematic than it has been considered till now: if (following Glarean) a *deviation* can be perceived by the listener, this can only mean that the same listener has been (and still is) able to form an idea of the modal quality that has governed the piece up to that point.

---

59. Finscher, "Zur Cantus-Firmus Behandlung"; Macey, "Josquin as Classic"; Finscher, "*Auss sunderem Lust*"; Steele, "Tonal Coherence."

60. Judd, "Aspects of Tonal Coherence," 54.

61. Meier, "The Musica Reservata," 75.

62. Glarean, *Dodecachordon*, lib. II, cap. 35, 163. Glarean's assertion that *Memor esto* "ad Dorium constitutum, finit in e parvo" plainly refers to the fact that, in both endings, the Tenor's last note is an *E* in the higher octave.

Example 4. Josquin, *Memor esto verbi tui*, mm. 319–28

As for *In principio erat Verbum*, apart from questions concerning its authenticity,[63] very little needs to be added to Judd's penetrating analysis, which refers to the gospel tone in order to make sense of the very peculiar structuring of tonal space noticeable in the piece.[64] While clearly terminating on F, *In principio* displays an astonishingly relevant role for D-cadences, a phenomenon Judd explains in the light of her theory of *ut-re-mi* tonalities. Let

---

63. Judd, "Aspects of Tonal Coherence," 253–54.
64. Judd, "Aspects of Tonal Coherence," 239–49, and Judd, "Josquin's Gospel Motets." The tone in question is the reciting timbre used in the mass for the proclamation of the gospel; it uses *fa* as a reciting pitch and concluding note, with downwards inflections to *re* for full stops and to *mi* leading again to *fa* for half closes and conclusion.

Example 5. Josquin, *Memor esto verbi tui*, mm. 142–65.

Example 5. (*continued*).

us recall shortly Judd's main points; 1) Josquin's structuring of the motet fits well both the textual and the musical character of the gospel formula on which the same motet is based; 2) the formula ends on F, but its main musical feature is the interval *fa-re*, so that the formula itself cannot be considered as an expression of the fifth mode; 3) within *In principio* five "melodic paradigms" can be traced,[65] which are "characteristic of modal types associated with a *Re* or *Ut* tonality,"[66] that is, a paradigm governed by a *semitone-tone* melodic descent (*fa-mi-re*) as opposed to one governed by a *tone-tone* melodic descent (*mi-re-do*). A *Mi*-tonality melodic pattern (*tone-semitone* descent) ending on A is however perceivable within the motet; its function, far from hinting at a transposed Phrygian, is to connect the *re* and *ut* types: "The ending on a *mi* in the tenor also suggest the way tonal coherence is organized within the gospel tone framework. A *mi* does not function as the final of the motet, but the *mi* type associated with it, which occurs frequently throughout the motet, connect the *re* and *ut* types spawned by the gospel tone."[67] If such is the musical situation, we then wonder whether, thirty years after Powers' deconstruction of modal theory, what Judd sensibly affirms is really at odds with the idea that the piece belongs in the fifth mode (or, in Glarean's terms, in the eleventh transposed *per bemolle*) with frequent *commixtiones* with the second. We think it is not, for the reasons mentioned in the last paragraph of this essay.

Before reaching any conclusion, however, let us consider one of the most challenging motets of all Josquin's output. Among his free-composed motets, the five-voice *De profundis* is by far the most problematic as to a possible modal attribution. Most scholars tend to point out the unrelenting continuity of the piece, its lack of internal cadences, and the unpredictability of its tonal plan.[68] The only serious attempt to describe the piece in modal terms has been by David Fallows, who once again had recourse to Glarean. The theorist's analysis of another *De profundis* setting by Josquin praised the ability of the

---

65. "The first (A) is directly connected with the gospel tone, but occurs as both *fa–re* and *sol–mi* third. [...] B is a subsidiary figure, subsumed in larger grouping. C is the rising third associated with section of motivic saturation. D, a *fa supra la* figure, occurs only once at the local level in the *prima pars* but several times in other section of the motet. E is the *ut–fa* fourth": Judd, "Aspects of Tonal Coherence," 248.

66. Ibid.

67. Judd, "Aspects of Tonal Coherence," 248–49.

68. Milsom, *Motets for Five or More Voices*, 305–6; Elders, *Symbolic Scores*, 139–40.

Example 6. Josquin, *De profundis*, mm.1–5.

composer to move from the Dorian to the Phrygian.[69] According to Fallows, "precisely the same happens in the setting a 5."[70]

Actually, a more clear-cut Dorian beginning is hardly to be found (shown in Example 6), and, yet, the piece ends on an E sonority. Fallows praises the result of this procedure as a magical surprise: "the odd thing—in terms of Glarean and the matter of modality in general—is that until the last bars there is almost no hint of anything related to an E final [...] the magic is partly that the final chord comes as though out of nowhere."[71] If, generally speaking, the broad sonic impression one receives while listening to the piece fits well with Fallows' description, we would nonetheless like to propose a quite different interpretation of its tonal space: one that considers the Phrygian mode well implanted in the tonal structures of this complex motet.

---

69. Glarean, *Dodecachordon*, lib. III, cap. 25, 364: "Hic vero mihi quisque acriter animum intendat velim, quale huius cantionis initium, quanto affectu, et quanta gravitate retulerit nobis verbum De profundis, ut sane Modos illos e nativo loco, quemadmodum fere in his fieri alias solet, in superiora non dimoverit, compraehenderit autem utriusque Modi systemata: Quanquam phrasin mira, ac de industria quaesita raritate vehementer confudit, nunc saltum Lydij, nunc Ionici usurpans, donec per lenocinia illa pulcherrima, clam rependo, in Phrygium tandem ex Dorio labatur, non offensis auribus."

70. Fallows, *Josquin*, 343.

71. Ibid.

Example 7. Josquin, *De Profundis*. (a): Bassus I, mm. 3–8; (b): Bassus I and II, m. 8; (c): Altus and Tenor, m. 10

As is well known, Josquin's five-voice *De profundis* is characterized by a three-voice canon: the Superius starts the composition with the subject of the canon, and it is imitated after two *breves* by the first Bassus at the lower octave, and after four *breves* by the Altus at the lower fourth. The first aspect to be considered, in order to grasp the tonal structure of the piece, is the outline of the subject.

As shown in Example 7a, its first musical phrase (corresponding to the first line of the text) already contains all the features of a *commixtio* between Dorian and Phrygian: in fact, it starts on D and unexpectedly concludes on E. We wish also to call attention to the modification of the conclusion of the subject, as exposed by the first Bassus, in the part of the second Bassus (the lower line in Example 7b).

While the former descends stepwise, the latter leaps up a fifth, creating a harmonic progression of the intervals of an octave and a third. Such a device is widely present throughout the piece, always at the end of a text line, or at least of a syntactic unit, and it reaches in turn different degrees: thus, it can be identified as a means of concealing the inner articulations of the polyphonic flow. We find this same device lightly presented after the first Bassus conclusion of the first subject, this time between Altus and Tenor (Example 7c). In both cases, the upper voice descends by a half step—which means that the linear clause of the main voice is a typical Phrygian one. The move from Dorian to Phrygian could not be more evident.

Example 8. Josquin, *De Profundis*, Bassus I. (a) mm. 82–94; (b) mm. 100–104.

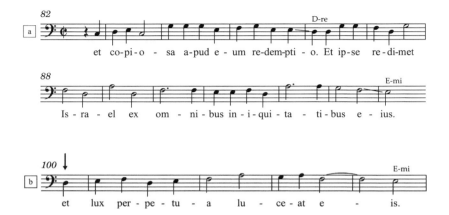

In addition, there is another important aspect to be considered. The text of the whole motet is made up of three (or even four, considering the final hint to *Pater noster*) different liturgical texts: Psalm 129 (130 in the Hebrew numbering), the introit *Requiem aeternam*, and the acclamation *Kyrie/Christe eleison*. Had the polyphonic writing been more traditional, there would probably have been subdivisions into three *partes*; however, this is not the case here. And yet, both the first and the second text end with clear-cut Phrygian linear clauses. Besides, both conclusions, each considered as a whole, display again the same modal shift of the beginning (Examples 8a and 8b).

As for the very conclusion of the piece, we must note that the ending on D of the first statement of the Kyrie on the part of the canonic Cantus is openly contradicted by the octave-third progression on G–B between the Tenor and the second Bassus which denies any possible Dorian interpretation of the conclusion (Example 9).

To sum up: we are in complete agreement with David Fallows in considering the shift from Dorian to Phrygian as the main modal characteristic of Josquin's five-voice *De profundis*, as well as with his consideration of the last sonority of the motet as somewhat surprising. But, at the same time, we are also convinced that the Phrygian mode, far from being unrelated to the inner structure of this complex and intricate polyphony, permeates it from the beginning of the piece. Moreover (and more generally), we believe that in such cases surprises are possible only 'against expectations'; therefore, we can assume a certain modal consciousness on the part of Josquin's contemporary listeners.

Example 9. Josquin, *De Profundis*, mm. 104–8.

Just a few words to conclude our analysis with two wide-ranging statements.

First conclusion: the analytical considerations, in our opinion, seem to confirm clearly enough that different resistances of the various tonal types to modal representation are to be found in Josquin's (sacred) music. Moreover, these different resistances appear to be generally in line with the ones noted in the work of later Renaissance composers. As far as modal representation is concerned, ♭–G and ♭–F are usually plain types; ♮–A and ♭–D most of the time highly problematic, and ♮–E and ♮–G (this latter as representative of the eighth mode) somehow fluctuating between the two extremes. This sequence, thus, corroborates the idea that such differences in tonal-type behaviours are related more to the intrinsic conformation of the musical material they organize than to the personal manner with which individual composers handle precisely that musical material. In Josquin, if anything, the boundaries between the different levels of resistance seem sometimes more subtle and less definite than in composers of the second half of the century: but, on closer reflection, this it is not surprising, since even modal usage evolves and (*pace* Powers) becomes more stable and more standardized across the Cinquecento (possibly thanks to an increasingly widespread 'internal view' of the modal system by the composers and to cross-fertilization between music theory and music practice). On the other hand, the commonest explanation for an example of a tonal type that appears to be counter-intuitive in its unusual resistance to modal representation—as is the case, here, of *In principio erat Verbum* with its high problematic ♭–F—is either a planned presentation of a rhetorical/exegetical intention by the composer (intending to express the sense of a particular textual meaning by means of special musical/modal features[72]) or the use of an extraordinary music configuration which in itself falls outside the modal system. This second scenario is exactly what happens in *In principio*, which is based on the gospel tone, i.e. on a tune that does not belong to any mode and whose un-modal properties can be exploited by the composer in order to connect modal regions normally distant from one another. (Of course, Josquin is not the only composer to use in such a way a reciting tone, and other instances can be found in the early as well as in the late Renaissance.[73])

Second conclusion: before turning to the consideration of the free-composed motet, we posed the question whether Josquin himself thought in modal terms while composing—a question whose answer, according to Judd, should be "it is unlikely." We think, rather, that at the moment there is no real answer to such a question—and probably never will be. Our intention, however, is neither to attempt a positive answer nor to contrast Judd's hypothesis. We believe, in fact, that there are other, more relevant questions concerning the relationships between modality and Josquin's polyphony that should be posed and answered. The first and foremost of these questions is whether a modally oriented analytical approach to this music may be considered as legitimate. Our analyses lead us to believe that a modal approach can indeed account for several important features of Josquin's motets, from both an analytical and a hermeneutical point of view. Nor are the numerous audacities displayed by his motets a good reason to dismiss such an approach: on the contrary, only a strong sense of 'tonal' coherence, such as that intrinsic to the modal concept, can favour a full perception of all deviations from the norms, and their communicative power. At the same time, in light of our references

---

72. For a case in point, see the discussion of Lasso's *Si bona suscepimus* in Sabaino "Lasso's Motets," 46–47.

73. For a later instance by a musician whose modal choices are most of the time easy to detect, one can examine Marc'Antonio Ingegneri's *Pater Noster* contained in the *Sacrae Cantiones cum quatuor vocibus liber primus* published in 1586: see the discussion of the piece in the "Introduction" to the modern critical edition of the motets (by Daniele Sabaino), 41–42.

to such prime theorists as Aron, Glarean, and Zarlino, we would invoke a full historic legitimacy for the modal approach, since their theories seem to have been forged precisely in order to explain at their best Josquin's music and that of his contemporaries. We could go further, to say that a modally oriented analytical approach to Josquin's music should be considered perfectly legitimate because it was Josquin's tonal-organising usage that gave birth to Renaissance modal theory, and not that a new theory preposterously 're-read' Josquin's music in terms of modality.[74] Renaissance modal theory, then, far from being, at one extreme, a normative constraint for composers or, at the other, foreign to their musical invention, should still be taken as a serious attempt to interpret and appreciate that music. After thirty years of deconstruction, it is thus time to reconsider what we can learn from that theory, not as a burden, but as a positive tool towards an always-deeper understanding of that wonderful music.

---

74. In these sense, our conclusion differs significantly from the assumptions that govern Powers "Is Mode Real?"

Bibliography

Antiphonaire monastique, 13. siècle: Codex F. 160 de la Bibliothèque de la Cathédrale de Worcester. Solesmes: 1922 (facs. repr. Berne, 1971 [*Paléographie musicale*, 12]).

Antiphonale Monasticum pro diurnis horis juxta vota RR. DD. Abbatum congregationum confoederatarum Ordinis Sancti Benedicti a Solesmensibus monachis restitutum. Editio kalendario accomodata congregationis Sancti Petri de Solesmis. Paris, 1939.

Aron, Pietro. *Trattato della natura et cognitione di tutti gli tuoni di canto figurato non da altrui più scritti.* Venezia: per maestro Bernardino de Vitali, 1525. Facsimile edition, Bologna: Forni, 1970.

Benthem, Jaap van. "A Triumph of Symbiosis: Angelo Poliziano, Josquin des Prez, and the Motet O *Virgo Prudentissima.*" In *The motet around 1500. On the relationship of imitation and text treatment*, edited by Thomas Schmidt-Beste, 409–507. Tours: Centre d'Études Superieures de la Renaissance, 2012.

Calvisius, Sethus. *Exercitationes musicae duae. Quarum prior est, de modis musicis, quos vulgo Tonos vocant, recte cognoscendis, et dijudicandis. Posterior, de initio et progressu Musices, alijsque rebus eo spectantibus.* Leipzig: Apelius, 1600. Facsimile edition, Hildesheim: Olms, 1973.

Corpus Antiphonalium Officii, vol. 2, *Manuscripti cursus monasticus*, edited by René-Jean Hesbert. Roma: Herder, 1965.

Elders, Willem. *Symbolic Scores: Studies in the Music of the Renaissance.* Leiden: Brill, 1994.

———. "Zusammenhänge zwischen den Motetten *Ave nobilissima creatura* und *Huc me sydereo* von Josquin des Prez." *Tijdschrift van de Vereniging voor Nederlandse Muziekgeschiedenis* 21 (1971), 67–73.

Fallows, David. *Josquin.* Turnhout: Brepols; and Tours: Centre d'Études Superieures de la Renaissance, 2009.

Finscher, Ludwig. "...*auss sunderem Lust zu den überschönen Worten*: zur Psalmkomposition bei Josquin Desprez und seiner Zeitgenossen." In *Literatur, Musik und Kunst im Übergang vom Mittelalter zur Neuzeit*, edited by Hartmud Boockman, 246–61. Göttingen: Vandenhoeck & Ruprecht, 1995.

———. "Four-Voice Motets." In *The Josquin Companion*, edited by Richard Sherr, 249–79. Oxford: Oxford University Press, 2000.

———. "Zur Cantus-Firmus Behandlung in der Psalm-Motette der Josquinzeit." In *Hans Albrecht in memoriam. Gedenkschrift von Freunden und Schülern*, edited by Wilfride Brennecke and Hans Haase, 55–62. Kassel: Bärenreiter, 1962.

Freeman, Daniel E. "On the Origins of the *Pater noster–Ave Maria* of Josquin des Prez." *Musica Disciplina* 45 (1991), 169–219.

Glarean, Heinrich. *Dodecachordon*. Basel: Heinrich Petri, 1647 (facs. repr. Hildesheim: Olms, 1970).

Hoffmann, Eucharius. *Doctrina de tonis seu modis musicis . . . ex vetustissimis musicis . . . conscripta*. Greifswald: Ferber, 1582.

Ingegneri, Marc'Antonio. *Sacrae cantiones cum quatuor vocibus liber primus*, critical edition by Daniele Sabaino. Livorno: Sillabe, 2014.

Judd, Cristle Collins. "Aspects of Tonal Coherence in the Motets of Josquin." PhD diss., King's College, University of London, 1993.

———. "Josquin des Prez: *Salve regina* (à 5)." In *Models of Musical Analysis: Music before 1600*, edited by Mark Everist, 114–53. Oxford: Blackwell, 1992.

———. "Josquin's Gospel Motets and Chant-Based Tonality." In *Tonal Structures in Early Music*, edited by Cristle Collins Judd, 109–54. New York and London: Garland, 1998.

———. "Reading Aron Reading Petrucci: the Music Examples of the *Trattato della natura et cognitione di tutti gli tuoni* (1525)." *Early Music History* 14 (1995), 121–52.

———. *Reading Renaissance Music Theory: Hearing with the Eyes*. Cambridge: Cambridge University Press, 2000.

———. "Renaissance modal theory: theoretical, compositional, and editorial perspectives." In *The Cambridge History of Western Music Theory*, edited by Thomas Christensen, 364–406. Cambridge: Cambridge University Press, 2003.

Krantz, Steven C. "Rhetorical and Structural Functions of Mode in Selected Motets of Josquin des Prez." PhD diss., University of Minnesota, 1989.

Macey, Patrick. "Josquin and Musical Rhetoric: *Miserere mei, Deus*, and other motets." In *The Josquin Companion*, edited by Richard Sherr, 485–530. Oxford: Oxford University Press, 2000.

—. "Josquin as Classic: *Qui habitat, Memor esto*, and Two Imitations Unmasked." *Journal of the Royal Musical Association* 118 (1993), 1–43.

Macey, Patrick and Jeremy Noble. "Josquin (Lebloitte dit) des Prez [Josse, Gosse, Joskin, Jossequin, Josquinus, Jodocus, Judocus, Juschino; Desprez, des Près, des Prés, de Prés, a Prato, de Prato, Pratensis]." In *The New Grove Dictionary of Music and Musicians*, 2nd ed., edited by Stanley Sadie, vol. 13, 221–66. London: McMillan, 2001.

Mangani, Marco. "L'organizzazione dello spazio sonoro nelle *Canzonette a tre voci . . . libro secondo* di Giuliano Paratico." In *Rinascimento musicale bresciano. Studi sulla musica e la cultura a Brescia dal Quattrocento al Seicento*, edited by Maria Teresa Rosa Barezzani, Antonio Delfino, and Rodobaldo Tibaldi, *Philomusica online*, 15/1(2016), 601–20.

Mangani, Marco, and Daniele Sabaino. "Modo Novo or Modo Antichissimo? Some Remarks About La-Modes in Zarlino's Theoretical Thought." In Early Music. Context And Ideas, 36–49. Kraków: Institute of Musicology, Jagiellonian University, 2003.

———. "Tonal types and modal attribution in late Renaissance polyphony. New observations." Acta Musicologica 80 (2008), 231–50.

Meier, Bernhard. Alte Tonarten: dargestellt an der Instrumentalmusik des 16. und 17. Jahrhunderts. Kassel: Bärenreiter, 1992.

———. Die Tonarten der klassischen Vokalpolyphonie, nach den Quellen dargestellt. Utrecht: Oosthoek, Scheltema & Holkema, 1974. English translation revised by the author: The Modes of Classical Vocal Polyphony Described According to the Sources. New York: Broude Brothers, 1988.

———. "The Musica Reservata of Adrianus Petit Coclico and its Relationship to Josquin." Musica Disciplina 10 (1956), 67–105.

Milsom, John. "Analysing Josquin." In The Josquin Companion, edited by Richard Sherr, 431–84. Oxford: Oxford University Press, 2000.

———. "Josquin des Prez and the Combinative Impulse." In The Motet Around 1500. On the Relationship of Imitation and Text Treatment, edited by Thomas Schmidt-Beste, 211–46. Tours, Centre d'Études Superieures de la Renaissance, 2012.

———. "Motets for Five or More Voices." In The Josquin Companion, edited by Richard Sherr, 281–320. Oxford: Oxford University Press, 2000.

Molmenti, Francesco. "L'organizzazione dello spazio sonoro nelle Messe di Josquin des Prez." Master's diss., Università degli Studi di Pavia, Facoltà di Musicologia, 2009–2010.

New Josquin Edition. Utrecht: Vereniging voor Nederlandse Museikgschiedenis, 1987–2016.

Powers, Harold S. "Anomalous Modalities." In Orlando di Lasso in der Musikgeschichte, edited by Bernhold Schmid, 221–42. München: Bayerischen Akademie der Wissenschaften, 1996.

———. "From Psalmody to Tonality." In Tonal Structures in Early Music, edited by Cristle Collins Judd, 275–340. New York and London: Garland, 1998.

———. "Is Mode Real? Pietro Aron, the Octenary System, and Polyphony." Basler Jahrbuch für historische Musikpraxis 16 (1992), 9–52.

———. "Modal Representation in Polyphonic Offertories." Early Music History 2 (1982), 43–86.

———. "Modality as a European Cultural Construct." In Secondo Convegno Europeo di Analisi Musicale. Atti, edited by Rossana Dalmonte and Mario Baroni, 207–19. Trento: Università degli Studi di Trento, Dipartimento di storia della civiltà europea, 1992.

———. "Tonal Types and Modal Categories in Renaissance Polyphony." *Journal of the American Musicological Society* 14 (1981), 428–70.

Rifkin, Joshua. "Motivik—Konstruktion—Humanismus: zu Josquins Motette *Huc me sydereo*." In *Die Motette: Beiträge zu ihrer Gattungsgeschichte*, edited by Herbert Schneider, 105–34. Mainz: Schott, 1991.

Sabaino, Daniele. "Lasso's Motets: A Case Study in Different Layers of Tonal Type Problematic Nature." In *Early Music Context and Ideas* 2, 38–57. Kraków: Institute of Musicology, Jagiellonian University, 2008.

Sherr, Richard. "Chronology of Josquin's Life and Career." In *The Josquin Companion*, edited by Richard Sherr, 11–20. Oxford: Oxford University Press, 2000.

Steele, Timothy H. "Tonal Coherence and the Cycle of Thirds in Josquin's *Memor esto verbi tui*." In *Tonal Structures in Early Music*, edited by Cristle Collins Judd, 155–81. New York and London: Garland, 1998.

Werken van Josquin des Près, edited by Albert Smijers et al. Amsterdam: Vereniging voor Nederlandsche Muziekgeschiedenis, 1921–1969.

Wiering, Frans. "Internal and External Views of the Modes." In *Tonal Structures in Early Music*, edited by Cristle Collins Judd, 87–107. New York and London: Garland, 1998.

———. *The Language of the Modes. Studies in the History of Polyphonic Music*. New York: Routledge, 2001.

Zarlino, Gioseffo. *Le Istitutioni Harmoniche di m. Gioseffo Zarlino da Chioggia, nelle quali oltre le materie appartenenti alla musica si trovano dichiarati molti luoghi di poeti, d'historici, et di filosofi sì come nel leggerle si potrà chiaramente vedere* [...].Venezia: [Pietro da Fino], 1558. Facsimile edition, New York: Broude Brothers, 1965.

JESUIT IMAGERY, RHETORIC, AND VICTORIA'S *SENEX PUERUM PORTABAT**

ANNE SMITH

One of the greatest obstacles in the creation of moving performances of sacred music from the 16th century is our lack of knowledge in regard to both the social and the liturgical contexts in which these works were originally heard. At the same time, they are frequently stripped of their functionality by our performances of them in the concert hall. An examination of one of Tomás Luis de Victoria's motets in relation to the Jesuit meditational practices of his time gives us an opportunity for discovering what the devout were expected to be contemplating when singing and listening to works associated with a specific feast day. This in turn can give us greater understanding of the music's compositional structure, leading to new ideas about its performance.

It is Victoria's long-term connection with the Jesuits that make the choice of his motets so suitable for this enquiry. Born in 1548 in Avila as the seventh of 11 children of Francisco Luis de Victoria and Francisca Suárez de la Concha, he began his study of music as a choirboy at the Avila Cathedral under Gerónimo de Espinar and Bernardino de Ribera.[1] His classical education probably began at S Gil, a school founded in Avila by the Jesuits in 1554. With the breaking of his voice he was sent to the Collegio Germanico in Rome, a Jesuit institution whose primary aim was the training of young men for the German missionary priesthood. A substantial number of English, Italian and Spanish boarders were admitted as well to provide the funding necessary for running the college. According to Casimiri, Victoria was one of these *convittore*.[2] For at least five years from 1569, the composer was employed

---

* An abbreviated version of this text was first presented at a seminar entitled *More Hispano: Tomás Luis de Victoria in Rome and Madrid*, held at the Fondazione Cini in Venice, on 10–16 May 2013. My thanks goes to Pedro Memelsdorff for having invited me to the seminar.

1. The factual information in this article is taken primarily from Robert Stevenson, "Victoria, Tomás Luis de." I am also extraordinarily fortunate that Noel O'Regan agreed to read and suggest emendations for a draft of this article in advance of submission. Various biographical errors were thus excised from the text. Any that remain are, of course, to be laid at my doorstep.

2. Raffaele Casimiri, "*Il Vittoria*: Nuovi Documenti," 114.

as a singer and organist at the Aragonese church in Rome, S Maria di Monserrato. In 1571 he was hired by the director of the Collegio Germanico to teach music to interested boarders, calling himself a *moderator musicae*. In 1575 he was ordained as a priest. Thus his earliest printed works, the motets from the 1572 Gardano edition, were created within and for Jesuit circles in Rome.[3]

It has been argued that Ignatius of Loyola's *Spiritual Exercises*, together with all of the later translations and other writings based upon them, are an invaluable source of information concerning the nature of the imagery used by Jesuits in association with their prayers and meditations on Biblical texts. These images, in turn, give us an idea of the significance of the texts to musicians of the time. In her book on William Byrd's *Gradualia*,[4] Kerry McCarthy points out the significance of the *Spiritual Exercises* within the English recusant context, demonstrating how the book informed Byrd's musical practice.

The following will first present some general information about the meditational procedures suggested by Ignatius, leading to a discussion of Jerónimo Nadal's explanations in his *Adnotationes et meditationes* concerning the feast of the Purification of the Virgin Mary, then relating them to Victoria's motet *Senex puerum portabat*. Finally this information will be applied in a rhetorical analysis of this piece with the intent of providing a basis for a performance which reflects its affective content within the Jesuit context.

Ignatius, the founder of the Society of Jesuits, was a Spanish knight, who when wounded in battle at Pamplona in 1521 underwent a spiritual conversion which entailed a period of intensive meditation and introspective reflection (see Figure 1)[5]. Between 1522 and 1524 he wrote down a set of meditational procedures, *Exercitia Spiritualia* (or *Spiritual Exercises*), based on his own experiences, designed as a manual for those who guided other individuals through the four-week program, whose ultimate goal was an election, or decision about how the individual might best serve God.

---

3. Victoria, *Motecta, quae partim quaternis, partin quinis, alia senis, alia octonis vocibus concinuntur* (Venice: li figliuoli di Antonio Gardano, 1572). RISM V1421, with later editions in 1583, 1589 (Milan, and Dillingen), 1603 and 1604.

4. McCarthy, *Liturgy and Contemplation*.

5. The image is after an engraving by W. Greatbach from a print by an artist called H. Wiers. Probably Hieronymus Wierex is meant.

Figure 1. Ignatius of Loyola. From Wishart, *A Short History of Monks and Monasteries*, plate between pp. 260–61.

A meditation on one of the mysteries, such as the Purification of the Virgin Mary, has a threefold structure: the preparation, the meditation itself and a colloquy.[6] The preparation consists of three parts: first, one recalls the narrative, reviewing in one's mind the scriptural text concerning the mystery; secondly, one imagines the scene where the event took place, down to the smallest details; and finally, one asks for what one wants and desires from the meditation in relation to the Lord. In the meditation itself, one first observes all the people involved, seeing them all in relation to oneself, to one's own inadequacies, with the goal of gaining some profit for oneself. Next one observes, marks and contemplates what those people are saying, and—reflecting upon oneself—draws some profit from it. Thirdly, one observes and meditates on what they are doing, and why, recognizing that all of Christ's suffering is for oneself. Once again one reflects on this, drawing some spiritual

---

6. This structure is paraphrased from the contemplations on the Incarnation and Nativity on the first day of the second week of the *Spiritual Exercises*. A Latin and Spanish version may be found online as *Exercitia spiritualia* (last accessed 8 March 2014; and an English translation as *The Spiritual Exercise of St. Ignatius of Loyola*, (last accessed 1 March 2014).

profit from it. The meditation ends with what Ignatius termed a colloquy, a term that he used for the prayer at the culmination of an exercise.

For me, the word meditation connotes some sort of quiet period of reflection, so that it was with some surprise that I read of the emotional upheaval that Ignatius experienced in his devotions that he recorded in his *Spiritual Diary* in 1544, a time when the Society was going through a period of consolidation. He constantly speaks of weeping, as when he wrote the following:

> Después, al preparar en cámara, al altar y al vestir, con algunas internas moçiones spirituales y motiuas a lágrimas, y así acabada la misa, quedando en mucho reposo spiritual. En la misa lágrimas en maior abundançia que el día pasado, a la larga y con çerrárseme la palabra, alguna o algunas vezes así mismo sentiendo intelligençias spirituales, a tanto que me pareçía así entender que casi no había más que sauer en esta materia de la Sanctíssima Trinidad.[7]

> *(Later when I prepared in my room, when at the altar and while I vested, I had more interior, spiritual impulses and felt moved to weep. After mass I remained in great spiritual repose. During mass the tears were more copious than the previous day and lasted continuously. Occasionally my power of speech was cut off. Once, or perhaps a few times, I felt spiritual intuitions so great that I seemed to understand that almost nothing more could be known on the subject of the Blessed Trinity.)*[8]

That this is not an exaggeration is perhaps shown by various images of Ignatius which have tears running down his cheeks, as can be seen if you look at Figures 1 and 2 carefully. It is also an indication, however, that, at that time, a greater degree of overt emotional expression was considered acceptable within the Catholic church than we—constrained by the religious conventions of our time—would expect. And in this context John O'Malley's assessment of Jesuit spirituality makes sense; that it, although it is rationalistic in its language and arguments, [it] is more profoundly concerned with right affectivity; while being logical in the organization of its parts, it is more profoundly psychological in its movement and design; and while being methodical in the aids it provides to prayer and spiritual discernment, it is more profoundly nonprescriptive in the outcome it foresees for the direct divine intervention that is its basic premise.[9]

---

7. *Monumenta Ignatiana, series tertia*, 102.
8. *Saint Ignatius of Loyola: Personal Writings*, 83.
9. John O'Malley, "Early Jesuit Spirituality," 6.

Figure 2. Detail of Portrait of Saint Ignatius of Loyola by Peter Paul Rubens. Photo courtesy of Norton Simon Art Foundation.

* * * *

With this as introduction, let us now turn to the visual aids for meditation created by Jerónimo Nadal. Although Nadal first met Ignatius in Paris in 1532, he originally was skeptical of the newly-founded community, not trusting Ignatius' motivation. It was not until 1545 that he joined the Society of Jesus, where he soon became the second hand of the first Father General. It was Ignatius himself who encouraged Nadal to assemble a guide to the spiritual meditations, including images and texts for each of the meditations. Although Nadal wrote the texts, designed the layout, and commissioned the 153 illustrations, the images first appeared posthumously in 1593 in *Evangelicae Historiae Imagines*, followed by larger editions entitled *Adnotationes et Meditationes* in 1594 and 1595, which included the Biblical texts as well as Nadal's annotations and meditations.[10]

---

10. Gerónimo Nadal, *Adnotationes et Meditationes*.

In order to demonstrate the potential this material has to enhance our understanding of the music of this period, I intentionally selected a motet by Victoria in which there seemed to be a discrepancy between its rather simple text and its emotionally-charged, chromatic musical setting, *Senex puerum portabat*. Its text is a concise description of the significance of the Feast of the Purification of the Virgin Mary:

> Senex puerum portabat: puer autem senem regebat: quem virgo peperit, et post partum virgo permansit: ipsum quem genuit, adoravit
>
> (The old man carried the child, but the child ruled the old man; him whom the Virgin brought forth, and after childbirth remained a virgin him whom she bore, she adored.)[11]

In envisaging what a polyphonic composition based on this text might look like, I would perhaps have expected longer note values for "The old man carried the child" (*Senex puerum portabat*) followed by fairly strict imitation for "but the child ruled the old man" (*puer autem senem regebat*), and increasing joy throughout the rest of the text (*quem virgo peperit, et post partum virgo permansit: ipsum quem genuit, adoravit*). But a mere glance at the dramatic opening of Victoria's setting (see Example 3, p. 145) shows that the composer had something entirely different in mind when he wrote the piece. The raised notes in conjunction with the octave leaps in all voices other than the alto create an emotional intensity usually associated with highly passionate or desperate texts. Let us see how Nadal's *Adnotationes et Meditationes* can help us understand why Victoria chose to set these words in this manner.

As with all of the meditations in the book, the chapter devoted to the Purification of the Virgin Mary commences with the narrative associated with the mystery, i.e. with the text from the Gospel according to Luke, chapter 2. As in the *Spiritual Exercises*, this is followed by a visualization of the scene, here in an engraving by Hieronymus Wiericx after a preparatory study by Bernardino Passeri, in which the individual events in the story are indicated by capital letters (see Figure 3). At the bottom of the page, there is a legend, so that one can follow the narrative in the illustration. This association is more elaborately described by the annotations on the following recto. And finally the section for the feast is brought to a close by the suggestions for meditation.

---

11. Translation by William Mahrt, Choral Public Domain Library, http://www1.cpdl.org/wiki/index.php/Senex_puerum_portabat. Last accessed 8 March 2014.

The passage from Luke 2 concerning the redemption of the Christ child as a first born, for five shekels and two doves as a poverty offering, provides the narrative context for *Senex puerum portabat*, within which the composition can be understood:

> Et ecce, homo erat in Hierusalem cui nomen Simeon; & homo iste justus & timoratus, exspectans consolationem Israel; & Spiritus sanctus erat in eo. Et responsum acceperat à Spiritu sancto, non visurum se mortem, nisi priùs videret Christum Domini. Et venit in spiritu in templum. Et cum inducerent puerum IESUM parentes eius, ut facerent secundum consuetudinem legis pro eo; et ipse accepit eum in ulnas suas, & benedixit Deum, & dixit; Nunc dimittis servum tuum Domine, secundum verbum tuum in pace. Quia viderunt oculi mei salutare tuum, Quod parasti ante faciem omnium populorum: Lumen ad revelationem gentium, & gloriam plebis tuae Israël. Et erant pater eius & mater eius mirantes super his quae dicebantur de illo. Et benedixit illis Simeon, & dixit ad Mariam matrem eius: Ecce positus est hic in ruinam & in resurrectionem multorum in Israël & in signum cui contradicetur; & tuam ipsius animam pertransibit gladius, ut revelentur ex multis cordibus cogitationes.

> *(And, behold, there was a man in Jerusalem, whose name was Simeon; and this man was just and devout, looking for the consolation of Israel. And the Holy Spirit was upon him. And it had been revealed to him by the Holy Spirit that he should not see death before he had seen the Christ of the Lord. And he came by the inspiration of the Spirit into the temple. And when His parents brought in the child Jesus, to do for him according to the custom of the Law, he also received Him into his arms, and blessed God, saying, "Now Thou dost dismiss Thy servant, O Lord, according to thy word: because mine eyes have seen thy Salvation, which Thou hast prepared before the face of all peoples: A light of revelation to the Gentiles, and a glory for Thy people Israel." And His father and mother were marvelling at the things spoken concerning Him. And Simeon blessed them, and said unto Mary His mother, "Behold, this child is set for the fall and for the rise again of many in Israel; and for a sign which shall be spoken contradicted. And thy own soul a sword shall pierce, that the thoughts of many hearts may be revealed.")*[12]

Figure 3 presents a sequential narration of the story told in the Biblical text, not dissimilar in layout to that found in a modern-day comic. Instead of presenting the details in textual frames and dialogue in balloons, as is done

---

12. All of the translations for the annotations and the meditation are by Frederick A. Holman, in *Jerome Nadal*, 171–73.

today, Nadal provided a legend beneath the illustration to lead us through the story. On the following page, he then provides further details, or annotations, to the individual letters, so that we not only can follow the story, but are also given additional information concerning the significance of the events.

> A: Templum, quo venit Joseph cum Maria matre Virgine & filio JESU, ut purificationis legem impleret cælestis Puerpera, simul ut redimeretur puer IESUS iuxta morem, tanquam primogenitus, etiam si lege neuter teneretur.
>
> (*The Temple where Joseph came with Mary the Virgin Mother and her Son JESUS to fulfill the divine law of purification after childbirth, and also, according to custom, to buy back as her firstborn the Child JESUS, even though the Law bound neither Mary nor JESUS*).
>
> B (at the back): Simeon iustus & timoratus, venerabilis senex, Spiritu Dei incitatus venit in Templum.
>
> (*We see Simeon, a venerable elder and a just man who feared God, [who] comes there led by the Spirit.*)
>
> C: [the prophetess]¹³ Anna præterea vidua ... ab excedra sua ... procedit ut Christo occurrat.
>
> (*Anna, a widow also inspired by the Spirit, [who] comes from her house ... to meet Christ.*)
>
> D: Ad primum introitum in templum fit obviam venientibus exultans spiritu Simeon. Accedit Anna, sistit gradum Maria virgo Mater gestans in sinu filium Dominum, consistit & Iosephus, complentur omnes divina cordis claritate ... Inclinat ex sinu matris ad Simeon læto vultu IESUS puer, commoventur interiora Simeonis, illum in ulnas excipit, augetur cordis eius alacritas, & splendor divinæ lucis; benedicit & celebrat divinam in se benignitatem, felicissimum item nuncium gentibus affert; nec his contentus benedicit Ioseph & Mariæ, laudis videlicet prædicatione. Huius verò cor perstringit prædictione Passionis Christi.
>
> (*A jubilant Simeon meets them as they come to the first Temple entrance. Anna draws near. The Virgin Mother Mary with her Son the Lord in her arms, stops, and Joseph, too. [All enjoy divine purity of heart.] ... A smiling Child JESUS reaches out to Simeon from His Mother's arms. Simeon's soul is moved, he takes*

---

13. Anna is referred to as a prophetess in the Gospel reading from Luke 2.

Figure 3. Hieronymus Wiericx, Feast of the Purification of the Virgin Mary. Engraving in Gerónimo Nadal, *Adnotationes et Meditationes* (Antwerp, 1595). Online edition, Bayerische Staatsbibliothek, 2 Hom. 372, (url: http://reader.digitale-sammlungen.de/de/fs1/object/display/bsb10144114_00147.html. Last accessed 21 November 2015).

the Child in his own arms, his heart throbbing in the splendor of divine light. He blesses and celebrates God's goodness to him. He brings the glad news to the Court of the Gentiles, and not content with that, he blesses Mary and Joseph in a canticle of praise. Mary grieves when Simeon predicts Christ's passion.)

E: Anna item ipsa ijs qui, quasi ad novæ rei miraculum, conveniebant bonæ voluntatis hominibus, atque in spe adventus Christi erectis prædicat Dei benignitatem, & adventus Christi mysterium.

(To devout bystanders hoping for Christ's coming, Anna preaches God's goodness in these events that herald the new order of things.)

F, G, and H: Hinc procedunt omnes versus santuarium primum ... Anteeuntem Simeonem spectabilem senem, puerum Deum brachiis gestantem contemplare; concipe quid operetur IESUS eius cordi adherens: sequitur Ioseph, consequitur virgo Mater & Anna, & alij pij Israëlitæ.

(All move from here [E] first to the sanctuary ... See how the venerable Simeon leads the way, with the Child God in his arms. Think what JESUS does as He rests on Simeon's heart. Joseph follows with the Virgin Mother, Anna, and other devout Israelites)

I: Perveniunt adianuam & Sacerdotes, offert Maria per Simeonem Sacerdoti ... puerum IESUM, recipitur oblatio, redimitur Dominator hominum & Angelorum, terræque cælorumque, quinque siclis ... quasi à morte ... numerat Ioseph Sacerdoti, Maria verò ex canistro alteri item Sacerdoti duas columbas, ut ex paupertate offert.

(The priests come to the entrance. Mary offers the Child JESUS through Simeon to them ... The offering is accepted. The Ruler of men and angels, of earth and heaven, is redeemed as a firstborn, as if from death, for five shekels ... that Joseph pays to a priest. Mary offers another one: two doves from a cage as a poverty offering.)

K: Hic etiam consitebatur Anna Domino, & loquebatur de Christo omnibus qui expectabant redemtionem Israël.

(Here too Anna praises God and heralds Christ to all who awaited Israel's redemption.)

L: Cum omnia secundum legem summa cum animorum consolatione perfecissent, ac Simeonis & Anne, & aliorum cordi omni suivitate replesset IESUS, & illis leto vultu extensa dextra benedixisset, reversi sunt in Galilæam ad civitatem suam Nazareth, eo scilicet iter ingressi.

(After they had fulfilled the Law to everyone's satisfaction, JESUS elated their hearts. With smiling countenance and His right hand raised, He blessed Simeon, Anna and all the others. Then the Holy Family returned to Galilee and their own town, Nazareth.)

After this complete, annotated version of the story, the topics of meditation to be associated with this Biblical scene are presented. Rather than placing the emphasis on the joy and the thankfulness towards this redemption of Christ, which in turn is a redemption of the faithful, one is asked to consider the following:

Eras tu quidem magne IESU, Dominus sabbati & legis, sed tamen factus es sub lege, factus es maledictum, factus es peccatum, ut nostra tolleres peccata O ineffabiles Dei nostri miserationes? Quid igitur mirum si nunc legem imples, eamque impleri etiam à Matre vis, qua non tenebamini? Redimeris tu quasi à morte quinque siclis, Mater duobus pullis columbarum quasi purificantur. Non fuit illa tui redemptio, etiam si fuit tuum meritum, sed nostri: non Matris illa purificatio, etiam si & hæc Matris meritum; sed nobis etiam ab ipsa in te & per te applicata.

Euge facte Puer, quos sanguine tuo redemisti purificà nos, ut Simeonem imitati te in ulnas cordis nostri recipiamus, ad pectus, & ad interiora cordis te foveamus & imprimamus. Hinc cæleste illud tuæ divinitatis lumen menti nostræ inseretur, revelabuntur tenebræ nostræ, te videbimus, te fruemur, quæ in mundo sunt omnia nobis præ te sordescent, ad te aspirabimus, dimitti ex hoc carcere desiderabimus, & tecum esse quando tu voles suavissime IESU.

(You were indeed, great JESUS, Lord of the Sabbath and of the Law. You were made a curse, even sin, to take away our sins. How unsearchable the mercies of our God! Is it any surprise, if You fulfill, and wish Your Mother to fulfill, a Law that did not bind You? You were redeemed from death, as it were, for five shekels, and Your Mother purified, so to speak, by offering two turtle doves. Meritorious as it was, that was not Your redemption but ours; if graced on her part, it was not purification of Your Mother, but it was for our benefit, in and through You.

Holy Child, You redeemed us with Your blood. Purify us, so that like Simeon, we may take You in our arms, to foster and impress You deep in our hearts. From there Your divine celestial light will flood our minds. Our darkness scattered, we will see and enjoy You. In Your presence we will grow weary of the world. We will aspire to You, and long to be free of this prison, to be with You, when You wish, dear JESUS. AMEN.)

The faithful are asked to consider all that Christ went through: he was made a curse, a sin, unnecessarily redeemed at the temple for five shekels, and died on the cross which will pierce Mary's soul "like a sword": all this to scatter the darkness in man's mind, for mankind's salvation. We are asked to mentally conjure up all that Christ suffered for the ultimate benefit of man, so that the faithful, like the Christ child at the temple, might be redeemed.

Although this interpretation may seem slightly exaggerated from this text alone, it is more comprehensible in relation to the *Spiritual Exercises*, taken as a whole. Indeed, Thomas de Villa Castin (1570–1649), in his book, *Manual de ejercicios espirituales* (before 1618), goes much further in this direction, as may be seen in the following excerpt from the first point of the twelfth meditation, "Of the presentation of the Child JESUS, and of the Purification of our Blessed Lady," in which one is asked

> Considera como la santísima Vírgen, quedando del parto de su Hijo mas limpia y pura que las estrellas del cielo, se sujetó á la ley de la purification, aunque no la obligaba y era con algun detrimento de su honor; y como si fuera una de las otras mujeres inmundas, llevó en compañía de su esposo á su unigénito Hijo al templo de Jerusalen [sic] para presentarle al eterno Padre y ofrecer sacrificios por él. Pondera cuán diferente entrada y ofrecimiento hace hoy de sí el Hijo de Dios eterno en el principio de su vida, de la que hará en el fin de ella; pues ahora entra en Jerusalen á caballo y llevándole la Vírgen en sus brazos, y despues entrará á pié, llevando él la cruz en que ha de ser crucificado sobre sus hombros; hoy entra para ser ofrecido en los brazos de Simeon, y despues lo será en los brazos de la cruz; hoy será ofrecido y redmido con cinco siclos, y allí será Redentor y se ofrecerá por amor de los hombres á los azotes, á la corona de espinas, á los clavos, á la cruz, á la muerte llena de dolores y afrentas: Saca de aquí un grande deseo de ofrecerte juntamente con este Señor al Padre eterno, para hacer perpetuamente su santa voluntad, y para llevar en pos de su santísimo Hijo tu cruz y trabajos; pues siendo él y su Madre la suma inocencia y pureza, se sujetaron á las leyes de los pecadores, como si lo fueran, con tales y tan heróicos actos de humildad; avergüénzate de que siendo tú tan inmundo y súcio, y un tan gran pecador, te ensorbebeces y deseas que todos te tengan por limpio, justo y santo.[14]

> *(To consider how the most B[lessed] Virgin, though after the birth of her dearest Son, she remayned more pure and immaculate then the starrs of heaven, did not withstanding subiect her selfe to the Law of the Purification, not being obliged*

---

14. Villa Castin, *Manual de ejercicios espirituales*, first published before 1618, when an English translation by Henry More appeared. Here quoted according to the edition published in Barcelona in 1858, 178–80.

thereunto; yea though in some sort it were preiudiciall to her honour. Wherefore as if she had beene like to other women uncleane, comming out of the stall of Bethleem, where she was delivered, in company of her Spouse, she carryed her only begotten Sonne to the Temple of Ierusalem, there to present him to the Eternall Father, and to offer sacrifice for him.

Ponder how different this entrance and obligation is, which the Sonne of God this day maketh in the beginning of his life, from that which he made in the end of the same: for now he enters into Ierusalem borne in the armes of the most Blessed Virgin, but afterwardes he shall enter on foot carrying the Crosse upon his sholders whereon he is to be crucifyed. To day he entreth to be offered in the armes of Holy Simeon: then to be offered in the armes of the Crosse. To day he shal be offered and redeemed with five sicles (a certaine coyne of that time) then as Redeemer, will offer himselfe for the love of men, to be whipped, crowned with thornes, nayled and crucifyed upon the Crosse, & to a most painefull & shamefull death. Gather hence great and earnest desires to offer thy selfe, togeather with this thy Lord unto the Eternall Fathers: alwaies to execute his most holy will, and to carry thy Crosse and the adversities which befal thee, after his most Holy Sonne: seeing that he and his Blessed Mother being most innocent and most pure, submitted themselves to the law of sinners, as if they had beene themselves also sinners, with such [and? almost illegible] so heroicall acts of humility. And be ashamed, seeing thy leife so foule and so abominable a sinner as thou art, to be so proud and haughty, desiring to be reputed & regarded of all as pure, holy, and just.)[15]

I quote these meditational passages in such great detail, as they shed a completely different light on Victoria's motet, *Senex puerum portabat*. They suggest, through the highly-charged writing with its rich use of dissonances, that Victoria was providing an aural vehicle for the devout in their meditations on all of the pain that Christ and the Blessed Virgin suffered for the benefit of mankind, and subsequent expression of thanks to the Virgin Mary for bringing Him into the world. We turn now to an examination of the rhetoric of motet's setting of the text against this background.

*   *   *   *

Although called into question by some Jesuit writers of the time, rhetoric was a central subject in humanist education.[16] By the middle of the century in both Germany and Italy, music theorists began to compare musical

---

15. Villa Castin, *A Manuall of Devout Meditations*, 215–17.
16. O'Malley, "Content and Rhetorical Forms."

works to orations, because their narrative structures were similar and their goal the same, namely, that of moving their audience. For example, according to Joachim Burmeister in his *Musica Poetica* of 1606, motets are constructed like an oration with an opening *exordio*, the body of the piece, and an ending. Each line of text has its own compositional device or rhetorical figure to express the affection inherent in it. What is fascinating about these lists of figures is that they are by no means restricted to "graces" or *mannerieren*, which ornament individual words or melodic lines, as one would expect from later theorists, but that many of them deal with structural elements of the compositions.[17] In his definitions of the individual figures he gives many examples, more than half of them from the works of Orlando di Lasso. Further he makes a rhetorical analysis of Lasso's *In me transierunt irae tuae* (from his *Sacrae cantiones*, published in Nuremberg in 1562) based on these figures.[18] It is the first published analysis of a contemporary musical work and gives insight into the relationship between the textual and musical structures from the perspective of the time. Although the remarks were intended for young musicians as an aid in composition, they are also invaluable to us today for they shed a different light on aspects of 16th-century style which we take for granted.

For example, both imitative writing and homophony were considered to be rhetorical figures, *fuga realis* and *noëma* respectively, and as such to be viewed from the perspective of how they express the text. Burmeister writes that the

> Noëma νόημα est talis harmoniae affectio, sive periodus, cuius habitus voces coniunctas habet in eadem sonorum quantitate, aures, imo et pectora suaviter afficiens et mirifice demulcens, si tempestive introducitur. Exempla sunt apud Orlandum in secunda parte *Exaudi Domine vocem meam* quinque vocum; in cantione, *In principio erat verbum*, ad

---

17. In his article, "Sonic Styles in the Music of Victoria," Daniele Filippi analyzes several motets by Victoria on the basis of the "sonic styles" used by the composer for the individual phrases of the text. His interest is to demonstrate that late 16th-century composers were using manifold compositional structures or "sonic styles" to give their works an audible form. Concerning his analysis of "*Vere languores nostros*," he writes "I have not dwelled on expressive aspects: but these strategies of articulation and differentiation, of symmetry and contrast obviously serve expressive as well as form-building purposes." (179) In the present article I am concentrating on the expressive aspects, but to use Filippi's words "they also serve form-building purposes."

18. For more on this analysis see Claude Palisca, "*Ut Oratoria Musica*"; Martin Ruhnke, *Joachim Burmeister*, 162–66; Gottfried Scholz, "Zur rhetorischen Grundlage von Joachim Burmeisters Lassus-Analyse"; Anne Smith, *The Performance of 16th-Century Music*, 102–30.

textum: "Omnia per ipsum facta sunt"; in *Nuptiae factae sunt in Cana*, etc. sex vocum eiusdem sub texu: "Et dixit ei Iesus." Observatio: hoc ornamentum, prout ornamenti partes explet, non ex nudis hisce exemplis notescet, sed ex ipso integri carminis contextu. Quocirca perlustrandus erit eius integer contextus, vel integra harmonia suis vocibus decantanda, ac tum demum se hoc manifestabit ornamentum.[19]

(Noëma is a harmonic affection or period that consists of voices combined in equal note values. When introduced at the right time, it sweetly affects and wondrously soothes the ears, or indeed the heart. There are examples in the second part of Orlando's five-voice Exaudi domine vocem meam; *in his composition* In principio erat verbum, *at the words "Omnia per ipsum facta sunt"; in his six-voice* Nuptiae factae sunt in Cana, *at the words "Et dixit ei Iesus." An observation: this ornament, inasmuch as it fulfills the function of an ornament, is made manifest not from these isolated passages, but from the context of the whole piece. Therefore the whole context must be examined. In other words, the whole piece should be sung by the voices, and then the ornament will reveal itself.)*

From the definition it is clear that these ornaments, these rhetorical figures, were not merely intellectual concepts but should be audible in performance. The example from *In principio erat verbum*, at the words "Omnia per ipsum facta sunt" (*All things were made by him*) from the Last Gospel of the mass, is presented in Example 1. This short homophonic section, lying between two longer, primarily imitative sections, enhances the meaning of the text by having the four lower voices declaim the words simultaneously, concisely, bringing home the message of God's creative power. It is a simple and effective way of expressing the content of the words.

A more subtle form of textual commentary may be found in the rhetorical figure of *pathopoeia*, which according to Burmeister is

figura apta ad affectus creandos, quod fit quando semitonia carmini inseruntur, quae nec ad modum carminis, nec ad genus pertinent, sed unius beneficio in aliud introducuntur; tum quando semitonia carminis modo congruentia saepius extra morem attinguntur.[20]

(a figure suited for arousing the affections, which occurs when semitones that belong neither to the mode nor to the genus of the piece are employed and intro-

---

19. Joachim Burmeister, *Musica Poetica*, 164–65.
20. Ibid., 174–75.

Example 1. Orlando di Lasso, *In principio erat verbum*, mm. 27–30. From *Sacrae cantiones, liber quartus* (Venice, 1566).

duced in order to apply the resources of one class to another. The same holds when the semitones proper to the mode of the piece are used more often than is customary.)

Example 2 is one of the examples of *pathopoeia* mentioned by Burmeister and is taken from the opening of the *secunda pars* of Lasso's *Quam benignus es*, at the words "O beatum hominem." Lasso's choice of a descending minor third to a raised note lying outside the mode for this text is striking, underlining as it does the sense of awe associated with a man protected by God. This is heard on a double level, melodically through the inflections caused by sharpened notes and vertically through the resulting "major" chords. In mm. 45–48, at the setting of these words, we are rapidly taken through a "modern" circle of fifths, a movement astonishing for the time, equivalent to the wonder connoted by the words.

Although no other theorist has so explicitly discussed the rhetorical relationship between the text and compositional devices in works of this period, despite the fact that the primacy of the text is mentioned by many, it has proved to be a very effective way of analyzing music from the second half of the 16th century, including that of Victoria. Furthermore, there are other

Example 2. Orlando di Lasso, *Quam benignus es*, mm. 45–56. From *Sacrae cantiones* (Nuremberg, 1562).

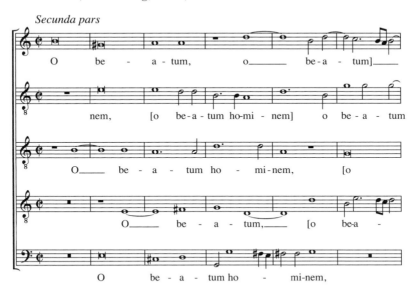

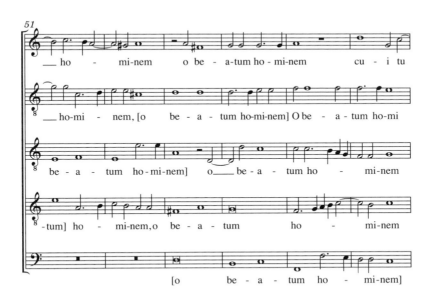

indirect links between Victoria and Lasso, in that the latter is known to have been in Rome in the early 1550's, and his works were known and sung there.[21] In 1556 he was employed at the court of Duke Albrecht V of Bavaria. In subsequent years we have documentation for connections between the Bavarian court and the Collegio Germanico. For example, in 1581, at the request of Wilhelm, the Fifth Duke of Bavaria, Walram Tumler came from the Collegio to teach the court in Munich the observance of the divine rights in accordance with Roman Jesuit tradition. In doing so he seems to have particularly irritated the court musicians who were under the direction of Lasso.[22] As Lasso and Victoria were both active in Rome—although it must be admitted that Victoria arrived there 10 years after Lasso had departed—it seems likely, given Lasso's international reputation, that Victoria would have been acquainted with his compositions; indeed it is difficult to believe that they did not meet when Lassus visited Rome in 1574. And whereas these connections remain in the realm of the hypothetical, it nonetheless seems appropriate to apply Burmeister's concept of analysis—given the pervasion of the sacred Italian style throughout Europe—to Victoria's motet *Senex puerum portabat* (Example 3).

The first section, the *exordio*, extends from m. 1 to m. 14, opening with a *fuga realis*, or imitative writing. The mode of the piece as expressed by the tenor and cantus is Phrygian, but is contradicted immediately by the inflection to G by means of the *F*-sharp in m. 3. This is then called into question by the C octave in the cantus and the turn towards a cadence in *a* in m. 6, which in turn is evaded by the movement to the *D* octave in the tenor and alto. The Phrygian sigh, on *e–f–e* at the end of the phrase in the superius makes it clear nonetheless that this is the modal center. Simultaneously the cadence on *D* is evaded by the lowering of the C-sharp in the altus and the progression to the G octave made by the lower two voices. These same elements are compounded by the denser writing at the repetition of the text in all four voices, by the cross-relation between *F*-sharp in the alto and *F* in the bass in m. 10, the *cadenza fuggita* in m. 11–12, where the raised note of the superius is a augmented fourth against the *d* in the alto and tenor, and the cadence itself is avoided by means of a 4–3 suspension in the tenor. It is not until m. 14 that we come to a place of rest on the final of the mode.

---

21. Thomas D. Culley writes that on January 17, 1583 Lasso's "*Deus misereatur nostri*" (from the *Sacrae cantiones ... liber quartus*, Venice 1566) was performed at the Collegio. See Culley, *Jesuits and Music*: I, 84.

22. Ibid., 90–92.

Example 3. Tomás Luis de Victoria, *Senex puerum portabat*. From *Motecta* (Venice, 1572).

Example 3. (*continued*).

Example 3. (*continued*).

Example 3. (*continued*).

Example 3. (*continued*).

Example 3. (*continued*).

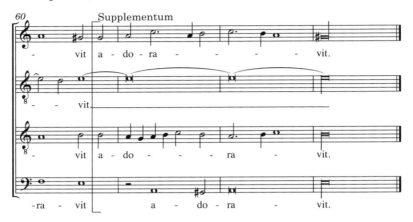

In contrast to the wonder associated with the use of *pathopoeia* in Lasso's *Quam benignus es*, here—together with the large number of avoided cadences—it serves to suggest an inner emotional turmoil or distress, and therefore would need to be brought out in order to encourage the listener to reflect upon all that Christ suffered in order to redeem his own sins. If indeed the goal behind the performance is to enhance the meditative process of vividly imagining the smallest details of the scene, an expressive performance would be more than justified.

The setting of the second line of the text, "*puer autem senem regebat*," the first affection in the body of the piece opens with a *noëma* in mm. 14–15, emphasizing the power of the boy over the older man. This device is then repeated in the superius, altus, and bassus in m. 16. The successive use of groups of voices in this manner is called a *mimesis*. The prevalence of the semitone at the words "puer autem," may perhaps also be seen as a reference to the future sufferings of Christ. The *chiasmus* "Senex puerum/senem regebat" is reflected by the return of the opening motive with its emotional ambivalence in the superius in m. 18. Here, too, we have a *cadenza fuggita* in m. 24 before the section comes to a close in m. 26. This cadence is heightened by the 4–3 suspension in the superius and by the fact that it is clearly set off from the following section which concerns the Virgin Mary. Thus the mood of the first section is maintained throughout the second one.

Like the second, the third section opens with a *mimesis*, a repetition of a homophonic section with different voices. The effect here, however, is quite different. The quick reiteration of "*quem Virgo peperit*" has the effect of intensifying the emotional impact of the implication that a virgin bore a child. In m. 31 we are forced to move onto the next affection—in spite of the cadence between the outer parts—by the entrance of the following line of text, "*et post partum virgo permansit.*" Here the raised note in m. 31 creates a major third in the cadence while at the same time it is the beginning of a *fuga realis* on the opening *soggetto* in augmented note values, perhaps in response to the word "*permansit.*" Thus here too, we return to the same emotional world as in the opening. In m. 38 we have a cadence similar to the one in m. 31, and the text is repeated coming to a close on a in m. 42.

The concluding section brings an ingenious combination of homophony and polyphony. The tenor and bass simultaneously sing the text "*ipsum quem genuit*" to the cadence formula at the interval of the third with a quasi-cadence on a at the beginning of 46. This melodic fragment is then taken up by the upper two voices, in simulated imitation, with cadences on *e* and *a* in m. 47. At that point the upper voice continues on, soaring up to the *e″* in a gracious melisma in m. 48, accompanied by *fauxbourdon* in the lower three voices, leaving the top voice alone in its quiet exultation. After the comparative coldness of the cadence on E, all the voices declaim "*adoravit*" together in m. 50 with an abrupt shift to a C major chord, creating an atmosphere of emotional warmth. The same process is followed for the text repetition in m. 53, with the alto and tenor beginning in thirds, followed by imitative entrances of the cantus and bassus. This time, however, the lower voices immediately join in the soaring joy of the cantus and continue in jubilation while it slowly descends above them. They all meet at the cadence on E in m. 60. This is followed by a *supplementum* or coda, which vacillates between *e* and *a* as is typical for compositions in Phrygian, before coming to a close on the final of the mode. Thus this final section, following the contemplation of the sorrow and pain suffered by Jesus and Mary for our redemption, expresses the gratitude and joy that they did this for mankind.

Our task as performers is to make use of these structural rhetorical devices to bring out the affective qualities. To do this we need to take the further step of translating Victoria's affective world into our own, finding parallels of emotional expression in contemporary life. Thus the *Spiritual Exercises* of Ignatius and Nadal can give us a new window for understanding the affective content of the music, opening up new possibilities, new choices of how to perform these works today. It demonstrates the necessity of further exploration of highly-expressive styles of performance for this repertoire, thereby replacing the ideal of ascetic purity that has reigned so long over this genre with the goal of touching the audience's hearts.

Bibliography

Burmeister, Joachim. *Musica Poetica*, Rostock, 1606. Edition and translation by Benito V. Rivera, as *Joachim Burmeister: Musical Poetics*, New Haven, 1993.

Casimiri, Raffaele. "Il Vittoria: Nuovi Documenti per una biografia sincera di Tommaso Ludovico de Victoria." *Note D'Archivio per la storia musicale* 11 (1934), 111–68.

Culley, Thomas D. *Jesuits and Music*: I. St. Louis, MO, 1970.

Filippi, Daniele. "Sonic Styles in the Music of Victoria." *Revista de Musicología* 35 (2012), 155–82.

Ignatius of Loyola. *Exercitia spiritualia; cum versione literali ex autographo Hispanico, notis illustrata*, Rome, 1870, http://babel.hathitrust.org/cgi/pt?id=hvd.hnpb8w;view=1up;seq=5. Last accessed 8 March 2014. English translation by Father Elder Mullan, S.J., as *The Spiritual Exercise of St. Ignatius of Loyola*, www.jesuit.org/jesuits/wp-content/uploads/The-Spiritual-Exercises-.pdf.

———. *Monumenta Ignatiana, series tertia: Sancti Ignatii de Loyola: Constitutiones societatis Jesu, tomus primus: Monumenta constitutionum praevia*. Rome, 1934.

———. *Saint Ignatius of Loyola: Personal Writings*, translated and edited by Joseph A. Munitz and Philip Endean. London, 1996.

McCarthy, Kerry. *Liturgy and Contemplation in Byrd's Gradualia*. New York, 2007.

Nadal, Gerónimo. *Adnotationes et Meditationes*. Antwerp, 1595. Online edition, Bayerische Staatsbibliothek, 2 Hom. 372, (url: http://reader.digitale-sammlungen.de/resolve/display/bsb10144114.html. Accessed 21 November 2015). Selections of the book appear in facsimile in *Annotations and Meditations on the Gospels*, translated and edited by Frederick A. Homann, S.J., Philadelphia, 2003.

———. *Jerome Nadal, Annotations and Meditations on the Gospels*, translated by Frederick A. Holman. Philadelphia, 2003.

O'Malley, John. "Content and Rhetorical Forms in Sixteenth-Century Treatises on Preaching." In *Religious Culture in the Sixteenth Century: Preaching, Rhetoric, Spirituality and Reform*, iii, 239–252. Aldershot, 1993.

———. "Early Jesuit Spirituality: Spain and Italy." In *Religious Culture in the Sixteenth Century*, IX, 3–27. Aldershot, 1993.

Palisca, Claude. "Ut Oratoria Musica: The Rhetorical Basis of Musical Mannerism." In *The Meaning of Mannerism*, edited by Franklin W. Robinson and Stephen G. Nichols, Jr., 37–67. Hanover, NH, 1972.

Ruhnke, Martin. *Joachim Burmeister: ein Beitrag zur Musiklehre um 1600*. Kassel, 1955.

Scholz, Gottfried. "Zur rhetorischen Grundlage von Joachim Burmeisters Lassus-Analyse: Ein Beitrag zur Frühgeschichte der Musikanalytik." In *Zur Geschichte der musikalischen Analyse*, edited by Gernot Gruber, 23–43. Laaber, 1996.

Smith, Anne. *The Performance of 16th-Century Music: Learning from the Theorists.* New York, 2011.

Stevenson, Robert. "Victoria, Tomás Luis de." Grove Music Online, http://www.oxfordmusiconline.com:80/subscriber/article/grove/music/29298.

Victoria, Tomás Luis de. *Motecta, que partim quaternis, partim quinis, alia senis, alia octonis vocibus concinuntur.* Venice, 1572 (RISM V1421).

Villa Castin, Tomás de. *Manual de ejercicios espirituales.* Barcelona, 1858.

———. *A Manuall of Devout Meditations and Exercises*, translated by Henry More. Second (?) edition: Liege, 1623.

Wishart, Alfred Wesley. *A Short History of Monks and Monasteries.* Trenton, NJ, 1900.

MUSICA DISCIPLINA

A YEARBOOK OF THE HISTORY OF MUSIC

VOLUME LIX, 2014

Edited by
STANLEY BOORMAN

Editorial Board

Tim Carter	University of North Carolina at Chapel Hill, USA
Anthony Cummings	Lafayette College, USA
Mark Everist	University of Southampton, GB
Dinko Fabris	Conservatorio di Bari, Italy
Barbara Haggh-Huglo	University of Maryland, USA
David Hiley	Universität Regensburg, Germany
Karl Kuegle	Universiteit Utrecht, Netherlands
Birgit Lodes	Universität Wien, Austria
Laurenz Lütteken	Universität Zurich, Switzerland
Anne MacNeil	University of North Carolina at Chapel Hill, USA
Anne Smith	Schola Cantorum Basiliensis, Switzerland
Anne Stone	CUNY, USA

Directions to Contributors

A full submission includes a cover letter, manuscript (with complete figures, examples, and tables), 250 word abstract, and a 50–100 word prose author biography.

1. Authors of articles to be considered for publication should submit one copy in digital Rich Text Format and a single complete hard copy to the editor at the address below.
2. Formatting should be kept to a minimum. All material should be formatted to fit on A4 or 8.5"×11" paper. Page margins should be a minimum of one inch (2.5 cm.) in all dimensions. Use a Times or Garamond font in 12 points and double-spaced lines. Please make sure that the text contains no hidden or extra returns, tabs, or spaces.
3. To allow for anonymous review, the author's name should only appear in the cover letter, which should also contain the full title of the submission and all relevant contact information. Authors should avoid identifying themselves in the manuscript itself (title page, header, footer, notes).

4. Supplemental materials.
   a. The submission should include a separate prose biography of the author's primary accomplishments, not to exceed 50 to 100 words in length.
   b. The submission should include a separate brief abstract written in English (max. 250 words) in conformance with the RILM guidelines and a list of works cited, following the bibliography style guidelines published by the *Chicago Manual of Style*.

5. All submissions should use the short style of citation in the text coupled with a complete bibliographic list of sources cited at the end of the article, in conformance with the guidelines given in *The Chicago Manual of Style*.

6. All musical examples, illustrations, tables, and figures, and other artwork should be submitted on separate pages following the article. Locations of all examples, tables, or figures should be clearly indicated in the text. (E.g. "Set figure 1 about here.")
   a. Musical examples should be submitted on separate pages, and they should be provided with underlaid texts and clear captions exactly as they are to appear in the article. Submissions originally created in Finale™ or Sibelius™ are especially encouraged, and we may request your original digital files if your article is accepted.
   b. Continuous tone and line illustrations are called "figures." Glossy positive photographs or scans at a minimum of 300 dpi at 100% of original size (uncompressed TIFF, PDF, or EPS) should be supplied for all continuous tone illustrations. You will be contacted if submitted artwork needs to be submitted in a different format.
   c. Please be sure that complete captions for all tables, illustrations, figures, etc. are provided on a separate sheet following the article, double-spaced.

7. Type is available for a large number of special music symbols, but fully notated music should not be included within sentences in the text of articles. Such notation is best included as examples.

8. Full submissions (cover letter, article, abstract, and prose author biography) can be sent by regular mail or by email with file attachments.
   a. If sending by regular mail, send a full hard copy plus a complete digital copy of all digital materials on a CD-ROM. Figures and musical examples can be sent as uncompressed TIFF, EPS, or PDF files. If music examples or other figures are written by hand, enclose a typewritten copy of any text that may be underlaid in the music. Send all materials to the editor at:

      Professor Stanley Boorman, Editor, *MD*
      Department of Music, New York University,
      24 Waverly Place, Room 268
      New York, NY 10003, USA

   b. If sending by email, send all electronic documents (Rich Text File) and in addition, a separate PDF of the full manuscript as an attachment. Include in the body of your email the cover letter, the brief abstract, and the single sentence biography. Send to: Stanley Boorman <stanley.boorman@nyu.edu>.

Musica Disciplina is published annually (Fall quarter) by the American Institute of Musicology, Verlag Corpusmusicae, GmbH, Münster, Germany.